THE PASSION TO HEAL

THE PASSION TO HEAL

Mike Endicott

Terra Nova Publications

© Mike Endicott 2003

First published by Terra Nova Publications Ltd, 2003

All rights reserved.

Mike Endicott asserts the moral right
to be identified as the author of this work.

No part of this publication may be reproduced or
transmitted in any form or by any means, electronic
or mechanical, including photocopy, recording or any
information storage and retrieval system, without
permission in writing from the publisher.

Published in Great Britain by
Terra Nova Publications Ltd
PO Box 2400, Bradford on Avon, Wiltshire BA15 2YN

Scripture quotations taken from the
Holy Bible, New International Version.
Copyright © 1973, 1978, 1984 by International Bible Society.
Used by permission of Hodder and Stoughton Ltd.
All rights reserved.

ISBN 1 901949 24 9

Printed in Great Britain by
Bookmarque Ltd, Croydon, Surrey

Contents

	Introduction	7
1.	Turning to the Streets	11
2.	Thinking Healing	22
3.	Choosing the Way	35
4.	A Question of Faith	47
5.	Authority and Sonship	61
6.	A Fiercely Burning Flame	76
7.	Into the Veil	86
8.	The Scribe Becomes a Prophet	97
9.	His Approaching Footsteps	107
10.	The Kiss of Tender Healing	115

Introduction

Jesus Christ has a passion for the healing of the sick and I have a passion to stand with him while he does it. I remain grateful to the medical profession for all that it does for us and I recognize that science was invented by God, but I ache as a Christian for those who suffer.

Great leaps forward in medical science have been granted to us in recent years. God reveals to his people his creative and re-creative power. But I have a strong sense that there is a mountain of healing blessing available which could be missed if the church fails to focus on the *power* of the cross.

We thank God for the contributions made to the body of Christ by faithful leaders and teachers in the church's ministry of healing evangelism, who point us to the word of God and encourage us to receive from him, according to his covenant promises, in the power of the Holy Spirit; but there is much to do, the well-known leaders are not called to do it all, and we need all hands on deck! So this book is written for those countless thousands of faithful men and women whose names are never in print, and whose faces are never seen in the church newspapers or on Christian television, whose quiet and unsophisticated toil in prayer bears fruit in the kingdom of God, and who want to see works of the kingdom of such magnitude that Jesus is glorified by everyone who comes to him. The so-called 'ordinary' Christian, who will not be singled out for any honour or attention, and is often hungry to see more spiritual fruit—more people coming to a personal knowledge of God, more people healed—is the one who can play a key role under God.

We tend to believe that effective Christian lives are not lived in the context of the ordinary, and yet the opposite is true. We sometimes focus too much on the high profile Christian—the writer; the person with the 'platform' ministry—and forget that 'great' Christian lives are only those which are subservient to the word of God. Jesus said to his disciples, "You are my friends if you do what I command" (John 15:14), and that obedience to him is what matters and makes the difference. Countless saints who started out along their road with Christ in quite ordinary ways are now numbered among the 'greats', and this only because of their obedience to God. The early disciples were simply ordinary people who became extraordinary because they fell into God's will for their lives. It really is the 'ordinary' people of the church who carry on the work of the gospel. We may think, quite wrongly, that our lives are much *too* ordinary for us to be effective in God's service, as we cope with jobs that may be less than exciting; our mortgages, and so many family and household needs, but the truth is that it is for *us*, in the midst of our everyday life, to heal the sick and to tell people that the kingdom of God has come near to them.

There is a great deal to do, and we should know what

INTRODUCTION

we are doing. We have to be about the business of the kingdom, but we should know our business and know it well. What most matters, though, is our relating to—and opening ourselves up to—our extraordinary God. He is capable of doing more for us than we could dream of, and longs to show us even greater things if we will work with him. How do we do that? Can we see greater things?

This book is not written to provide all the answers. Rather, these pages contain a contemplative stream of thought, not on how we might make him nearer to us in time of trial—for his power is already at work within us, and Christians are already the 'temple of the Holy Spirit' —but about how we might, as his servants, know more of his love and power as we serve him in the midst of other people's trials, becoming more Christ-like ourselves, and more transparent, more open to the flow of his goodness, so that the 'living water' of which Jesus spoke overflows to those in need. (See John 4:10).

These thoughts begin with my memory of a revelation of God's love imparted to a long-standing clergy colleague, whose walk into fruitful healing ministry resulted from that experience. We examine together two of the most widely accepted theologies of healing, and go on from there to build a third that looks to the possibility of our seeing 'even greater things than these'.

It is suggested that the expression of God's **authority** and **power** against illness is one important gateway for maintaining the flow of his power to heal the sick, in the context of an effective healing ministry. We shall see how such authority must be rooted in **sonship**, and in the corporate **faith expectancy** of the body of Christ.

The would-be effective minister of healing is encouraged to become a pilgrim, not, as it were, battling on through the apparently never-ending stream of other people's pain with God at his side, but rather turning through ninety degrees and journeying into the veil that lies between heaven and earth. It is here that the humble minister becomes infused with what is to be found there: grace, compassion, authority and power. Then, turning back, in humility, towards God's people with the authority that comes from such sonship, we discover that the power of God to minister effectively is freely imparted to those who would avail themselves of it.

And we, who with unveiled faces all reflect the Lord's glory, are being transformed into his likeness with ever-increasing glory, which comes from the Lord, who is the Spirit.
 Therefore, since through God's mercy we have this ministry, we do not lose heart.

2 Corinthians 3:18–4:1

Learning to flow in and reflect Jesus Christ's healing grace, so that we begin to be useful and effective in healing ministry, does not usually happen instantaneously! We have to grow in his grace, and there are battles and struggles along the way. Needless to say, it is not about confidence in *ourselves*, but, rather, confidence in, and personal knowledge of, *his* love and power. Such openness to his life-changing power can grow, perhaps tentatively at first, but then blossoming into a flower of ministry that brings praise to God. All the glory goes to Jesus.

1

Turning to the Streets

A young couple stood on the vicarage doorstep, politely requesting that they be given a guided tour around the picturesque Norman church across the road. My friend, the priest in charge, duly complied. One set of their grandparents, it would appear, had been married there three quarters of a century earlier, and the couple were in the area, checking up on their family roots. At the end of their guided tour, marked by many gasps of delighted surprise and wide-eyed amazement at the beauty and antiquity of the structure and its contents alike, they asked, "How many years ago did they last have a church service in here?"

Their words enveloped him like a grey rain cloud. A tidal wave of depression flooded over my clergy friend as the realisation dawned. His visitors (perhaps like many others) innocently assumed that his church was a museum, his guided tour a glimpse into a bygone age of an outdated spirituality, and he himself no more than the curator of a fine and ancient example of English architecture. Eventually, the visiting couple left, tossing a few coins onto a brass plate by the door, thanking my friend profusely for his time, commending him for his obvious caring for the old place. Closing the heavy doors behind his visitors as, hand in hand, they skipped and chattered their way down the sunlit path to the churchyard gate and the main road, my friend returned to his altar. There he prostrated himself on the ground before it, crying out for forgiveness, direction and grace. Was he, he wondered in prayer, over-reacting or had he caught the faintest glimpse of something very painful and disturbing to Christ himself?

Returning home, he exchanged his clerical collar for a casual shirt, and wandered around the nearby shopping centre for almost an hour, occasionally asking the busy passers-by for directions to his own church. No one could help him. Sometimes his question provoked a blasphemous response. But he knew that these were only poor, shrivelled and crippled ends of prayer, lost behind the words of those who knew nothing of the reality of God. Apparently, for some reason, they still appeared to find a need to speak of God, even if it was only through their clenched teeth. They certainly did not know how to find his church.

This gloomy picture felt even worse to him with the freshening realisation, and a sharpening sense of responsibility to those around him, that God still wants to use his body, the church, to offer to the world a perfect moral and spiritual model. Throughout all the many upheavals and changes of the past twenty centuries, his revelation of good news in Jesus Christ has been and still is the cause and source of passionate self-giving love.

So are we, the church, only a museum —or the holders of something which is very precious: the gospel of Jesus' love? This love, the true light offered to the world, has been seen in action in every age, and throughout the whole world; it can have a major impact on every nation, and in the midst of all political situations, as well as on all ages, temperaments and conditions of people. The three years of our Saviour's ministry on earth did more to regenerate and soften the hearts of mankind than all the philosophical discourses and all the exhortations of our secular moralists put together! Has all that love and power retreated? Can we still expect to find it at work even among our congregations?

That crowded afternoon in the shopping centre, my clergy colleague reached his Slough of Despond. A depressing weight had squeezed out of him all his enthusiasm for what he was suddenly recognising in his work as a sort of Old Testament priestly conducting of ritual. From that day on, he knew that things had to change. There had to be more: there had to be a way for him to move on. There had to be a place outside the walls of the church building where God would be recognised as who he is. There had to be for him, somewhere, a place where theory would break through into reality, and what many saw as just ecclesiastical rhetoric would become received, simple truth. Standing among the milling shoppers, slightly bewildered, his heart ached and cried out to move on from his religious place of only holding worship services *for* God but seeing no miracles, to a situation of working *with* God, who *actually does miracles*. Gone was the desire to merely *speak about* a God who wants to change his parishioners' lives; now he longed to see those changes occur and needy souls helped. He yearned for the cross of Christ to be recognised in these streets for what it surely is: not only the central symbol of Christian faith, but the powerful message of the working power of God. To hold out the healing light of Jesus Christ would mean reaching out. He knew that the commonly accepted flow of church life around him would probably be in the opposite direction —after all, the tendency of all religions is to care more for religion than for humanity. Jesus, though, cared more for humanity than he did for religion; his compassion for the needs of ordinary people seems to have been much more important to him than the customs and habits of the professionally religious people.

Standing in the swirling crowd, between the larger department stores, without recognising any of the shoppers, he became aware that the natural instinct of contemporary Christianity, for a myriad of reasons, is to find ways to soften Jesus' radical teaching and let his compassionate vision for all these folk drift out of focus. If Christians lose sight of these things—and he wondered if he were not in that exact place himself—the amazing message of Jesus would have very little impact on either our own lives or the lives of those we want to reach.

Then, inexplicably, his heart began to lift. We ought to know, in opposition to the world view, he reminded himself, that it is in Christ that the whole universal structure of things—including everything that goes on in the lives of all the people around us in the street—holds together. A large proportion of those who walk past us every day have lives that are falling apart, or have fallen apart, and it seems to many that there is nothing for them to do but live with it, without knowing the divine longing to piece them back together again.

For by him all things were created: things in heaven and on earth, visible and invisible, whether thrones or powers or rulers or authorities; all things were created by him and for him.

He is before all things, and in him all things hold together.

Colossians 1:16–17

Around us is so much that is in need of new life, and my friend was feeling at that moment, with a new and almost bold frustration, that the kingdom of God is full of the power that raised Jesus from the dead. Those of us who have begun to live in this kingdom dynamic know, as a direct consequence, that we are living in our Father's house; that it is a big and healing house —and that perhaps we have begun to explore only a tiny part of it.

As long as we keep the word and its author as our foundation and base camp, there is a long way to go from wherever we are. With him as our guide there is much exploring to do. This house has wide and distant horizons towards which we must travel, and some of them are still unfamiliar. But it is his house, all of it.

To be such an explorer, what should we do? How was my friend to approach a fresh direction and emphasis in his ministry? What frame of mind would set him right on the journey? What is the right attitude to adopt when we seek to follow his example? Jesus said,

"If anyone would come after me, he must deny himself and take up his cross and follow me."

Mark 8:34b

Would this be the new way forward for my colleague: to push self out of the picture? He knew full well that denying self is an intensely arduous thing to do. It is a very much more difficult proposition than it sounds. The more any of us denies self and turn outwards to the world, the more of self we discover there is to deny! Our innate self-assertiveness declares itself in the strident notes of our first infant shriek, and has a tendency to become stronger in us through all the various stages of life. In the kingdom of God, however, the opposite mind-set is required of us: we must be as 'barefoot pilgrims' and 'tent dwellers'. "You died," wrote Paul the apostle in Colossians 3:3, "and your life is now hidden with Christ in God."

Could healing and restoration of life be brought from heaven to the people in these modern times? Would all this be practically impossible to live up to? Is not the task of living as a Christian in the biblical sense—in accordance with the instructions of Christ to teach the kingdom and heal the sick—impractical in this day and age? Would it not be better to stick with the things he knew? Why not carry on his ministry tomorrow as he did it yesterday? At least that might avoid any further trials and self-denial.

Longing to see the sick and the troubled healed in the name of Christ, he related later, may be thought of as climbing into a boat which will take us somewhere; always surrounded by the wind and waves. It is true to say that there are few guarantees about the nature of the voyage; the ones that matter are the promises of God in his word, and we take hold of them by faith.

Jesus encourages us into his boat to travel with him to the other side of the lake. We must be prepared to journey with him from Christian territory into territory which is peopled by unbelievers, sailing out of the known into the unknown. We will go from the familiar to the unfamiliar, frighteningly drifting out of our comfort zones towards chasms of insecurity. We will fall from a place of safety in prayer into risk in ministry; from understanding our friends to listening to strangers; from theological comfort to struggle; from self-interest to selflessness; and we will die to self for the purposes of finding self and our true role in the kingdom of God.

But would it be worth it in the end? Would there be any real gain? Would this be just another massive church effort with few results to show for it, other than a degree of satisfaction for having at least tried? Would turning our hearts towards humanity first, and keeping our religion in second place, be a cultural upheaval that yields too little?

Hovering among the jostling crowd, their parish priest began to wonder if his new enthusiasm would soon die in the harsh light of day. He wondered whether, at any level, his message would be accepted by those around him. Would they just consider that life is life, and all we can do is to make the best we can of it under whatever circumstances it throws our way, since not much can be changed? That widely held belief militates strongly against acceptance of the gospel. There is, even among many Christians, an embattled sense of there being something essentially and inevitably unrecoverable, perplexing and mysterious about this world that we live in. There appears to most of us to be an unclimbable mountain of things we can do nothing about. We might till the soil on the hillside, but we cannot bulldoze away the mountain. There is a bulk of darkness which, however hard we may try, will never see light. The poor will always be with us and, unhappily, so will the sick. The world we live in seems to be a basically bad place —everything is so complex and beyond our influence, and we feel that no more can be practically hoped for. The best we can expect out of life is to get through it with some dignity, and some pleasures along the way. Of course, we continue with plenty of protests over all manner of things in the name of Christ, perhaps made in obedience but often with no real hope that any real, deep change will result from our efforts. There are many things that we do as a matter of duty, rather than conviction that our actions can make a difference.

There is little that is Christian about such an attitude! Uniquely, and unlike all the world's religions, the Christian faith is about a great change in the believer: a transformation; a movement from life under the dominion of sinful rebellion into new life in the kingdom of God, made possible by grace, and appropriated by faith in the sacrifice of Jesus on the cross. The idea that there will always be an unavoidable water table of tragic and painful circumstances assailing us, implicitly accepts the pagan view that there is, at the root of things, a sort of terrible maliciousness, which will eventually force us all down unwanted roads of personal tragedy unless some unknown and unseen gods can somehow be appeased. Christians need to stand outside that dark view. We have learnt something very different: we have discovered that all things were created by the eternal Word, namely Jesus Christ, and in him all things hold together.

In this light we should at least be able to see clearly the pitfalls that await us, and so easily trap us into lifestyles which themselves lead to sickness and despair. Christians, my friend presumed, among the pressing hubbub of parents and pushchairs, are born to be the real and active revolutionaries of our time. In his mind's eye he saw the church standing against the surrounding postmodern society's all-pervading belief that truth is relative, not absolute. What was right for most of those busy people around him, he assumed, would depend on what they wished to believe was right. After all, he thought, the words of Pilate — "What is truth?" — have a profound resonance for many people today. Peace with each other at any price means that, too often, we slip into maintaining the status quo instead of being radicals, solidly established against the shifting sand dunes of this relativism.

It does not have to be that way. What a marvellous thing it would be to see Christianity really and joyfully affecting these people's lives at the point of their need, touching them where it hurts. Surely, at least in modern industrial societies, that would be in the area of their ill health, above all else. Evil is evil and sickness is sickness, he concluded, and God hates it to the point of the cross. Christians, he assured himself, should not be living in museums, nor be so ready to go along with everyone else's world view that a certain amount of evil is inevitable, but, rather, should be the first into the field against what is wrong. Sickness is not God's will!

My friend searched around him for faces he could recognise in the crowd —there were one or two that passed him, but these were very few. Where, he wondered, had evangelism gone, that so few in these streets had been touched by the kingdom of God, or even wanted to be? Healing would not of itself be enough —a fine witness it may be, but we do not live in a thankful and God-centred society. Healing without evangelism would never achieve much for the extension of the kingdom. The early church did not separate these two ministries: evangelism and signs and wonders went together. No wonder we do not see New Testament results from our efforts today!

Such holy frustration was to lead him on to become a channel for the healing, life-changing power of the Holy Spirit, not because he was specially chosen for that purpose but because all Christians are; and not because he discovered any secret 'talent' for healing the sick. He simply fell into God's will for the church. Walking home again that afternoon towards the setting sun and his vicarage, one prayer was on his lips.

> O LORD, I call to you; come quickly to me.
> Hear my voice when I call to you.
> May my prayer be set before you like incense;
> may the lifting up of my hands be like the evening sacrifice.
> Set a guard over my mouth, O LORD;
> keep watch over the door of my lips.
> Let not my heart be drawn to what is evil,
> to take part in wicked deeds
> with men who are evildoers;
> let me not eat of their delicacies....
> But my eyes are fixed on you, O Sovereign LORD;
> in you I take refuge....
>
> *Psalm 141:1–4,8a*

As he strolled along the pavement, he began to see himself already in the daily evening disciplines of a pilgrim, gathering his thoughts, facing the very real possibilities of misunderstandings and opposition, reintegrating himself with God's will, in voice, hands, mouth, heart and eyes, and re-setting his course.

And it is not only that colleague whom God has called. Today the healing of ordinary lives takes place throughout many different countries and, within them, throughout every label of Christian spirituality and denomination. It can happen through anyone —sometimes through the clergy and sometimes laity. It happens in different settings: healing services, communion services, conference platform ministries; it can be at a hospital bedside, or the warmth of a country kitchen. It happens through the ministry of bishops and through the hands of newborn spiritual babes —in fact, through any Christian who has the courage, and sufficient expectancy of God, to try!

2

Thinking Healing

'...They will place their hands on sick people,
and they will get well.'

Mark 16:18b

In this one simple, staggering, inspiring sentence, Jesus Christ tells the world something amazing about his disciples then and throughout the ages which were still to come. They could heal the sick! They did not have any particular medical ability of their own—the authority and the power came from God—but they took the initiative and saw results.

"Lord," said the seventy-two, returning with joy from their teaching and healing mission, "even the demons submit to us in your name."

Doubters say that all those times have passed, but what happens if we do *not* want to doubt —if we want to follow Jesus in his ministry and help others, extending the kingdom of God and healing illness? What happens if we express a desire to heal the sick and to take joy in the results, as those early disciples did? Can we delight our heavenly Father and bring him pleasure by imitating his Son in healing the sick? Praying for people is one thing, but actually seeing them healed, that is quite another! My clerical friend, whose revelation for healing began one weekend afternoon in a crowded street, once taught me to look wide-eyed towards heaven and ask, 'Would it not be wonderful if it were true, that we could do such things today?' Other than the re-building of the broken temple walls of body, mind and spirit, what else is there in this life to be so enthusiastic about, exciting enough to throw one's whole life into it? What lifts the soul into such passion to see the sufferer free? What is it that makes the heartbeat stumble a little with anticipation at the very thought of it? The answer to these questions lies waiting for us in the imagination of the soul. Such flurries of the heart, such love-passion to see his glory fall, these sensations occur as our own spirits leap towards our God, greater and more encompassing than the universe itself, and yet stooping to touch an individual soul with the healing tip of a finger. And touch us he surely does!

When we consider God's mighty creation of the universe, of heaven and earth and the moon and the planets and stars he has placed above our heads, we have little option but to wonder at how precious to him we human beings must be, or how divine love has stooped to meet us. We can be assured that God is infinitely loving and caring toward each of us. His will for us is that we should be healed of all sickness and disease. He has made us only a little lower than the heavenly beings and crowned us with glory and honour. Compared with this generosity of God, what on this earth could mankind be, that the living God should make so much of us and pour out his love on us?

What can we know, then, of Jesus Christ, from our own experiences? We can know that he is alive, personal and real, and closer than we think. We may feel his presence. Many have felt his healing touch, and have seen the changes he has made in our lives, not just in lifting a mood or two, but in dissolving away confusion and doubt, melting our pride and persuading us to do the right thing —in other words, to be obedient. Most thrilling of all is the sight of him, or rather the strong and gentle effect of his power, as it brings his healing touch to huge numbers of people.

If we allow Jesus to reign in us, the Fatherhood of God is supreme, and we experience that as a living reality, not just a theological theory. We belong to him for we have become his children by adoption and grace, when we accepted Jesus as Saviour and Lord, turning to him in repentance, receiving him and accepting his sacrificial death on the cross as the price paid for our sins. Without him we would be absolutely powerless to do what we know we ought to do, to change our own character, habits or disposition, or to work with him to heal the sick. But he can change these things. He can help us to overcome any weaknesses or failures, real or imagined. Aware of our own inadequacies, we learn of the power that raised Jesus Christ from the dead that is now at work within us. We learn and experience his ability to change that which we are not able to change, providing of course that we are obedient to his leading.

It is also exciting and fascinating that the living Lord Jesus Christ should be interested in every detail of our daily lives. And why should this not be so? If he has numbered the hairs of our heads, if he notices the fall of a sparrow, would he not care about what we do every day, how we do it and how it hurts us? Would he not be interested in how well we are able to relate to other people, about our behaviour and our concerns for others? Would he not care about our illnesses? We cannot simply shake our heads and refuse to believe how *practical* God is. Nobody could seriously believe that the universe was made by God and at the same time fail to be persuaded that he takes care of those he loves.

Consider his immediacy, in being alongside us and dwelling in us! What should we say in an important conversation? If we will listen to him, the words will be there. If we will let him, he is practical as he helps us make those hard decisions in life. He will give renewed strength to the weary, if we will go to him. In the same breath we might affirm that the sick will be healed if we will lay our hands on them.

Healing the sick is not an expert ministry for the specially gifted. It is for all of us to 'try our hand', albeit hesitatingly, for while one person wavers because he might feel inferior, the other is busy making mistakes and growing in Christ because of them.

Although I feel today a poor pilgrim compared with so many others amongst God's people, I must confess that my great joy in life comes through the exercise of one special favour that has been allowed me: to teach into the church the bottomless treasure trove of Christ's healing love, and to attempt to explain, as plainly and simply as I can, this one particular mystery —that our Lord Jesus Christ is indeed fully God and fully man and that he sacrificially died to save us from the unwelcome consequences of sin: our iniquities, our illnesses and even from eternal death. He came to save us from them all. He did this in his death by exhausting the power of all the curses of this life. As with the bronze snake of Moses, the power that evil has over us was put upon him and was killed with him —not the evil itself, but the power that evil has to ruin lives through sickness. The passionate longing to see this great salvation as experienced reality is the driving force behind the church's healing ministry. Not a moment of Calvary must we waste in ignorance of it.

Nowadays I seem to find plenty that is senseless, depressing and downright bad in this world, and the world contains plenty of other people who would agree with me. Some have said that this proves that there is no God of love, and others that we inhabit a good world gone wrong. Somehow, strangely enough, we have a memory of what should have been. Somehow, in the deepest recesses of our unconscious senses, lies an understanding that the original design was perfect: the planet was made to be wholly like Eden, and we were made in the likeness of God himself; we were made to be Jesus-like, as were Adam and Eve, enjoying a perfect relationship with God. When attacked by any illness we may at first believe that God has some purposes in it, but our first and natural port of call is the surgery. There is something deep within us which tells us that it is not supposed to be like it is. We know that sickness is not right. Because of sin, because of our own in-built capabilities for sinning, we inhabit a broken version of the original, in both the planetary and bodily sense. We are a fallen race, with sin infested blood coursing through our veins. God did not create us to be this way; we were not designed to be broken by sickness and disease. This is the way that it so often is, but we know there is more, much more.

> In the beginning God created the heavens and the earth. Now the earth was formless and empty, darkness was over the surface of the deep, and the Spirit of God was hovering over the waters. And God said, "Let there be light," and there was light.
>
> *Genesis 1:1–3*

As we learn from Genesis, there had originally been a serpent-free paradise on earth. Man was created to worship God, subdue the earth and have authority over it. Disobedience entered creation, and the turmoil of sickness and death fell across the face of what had been perfect. We let the snake loose in the world, and we are all poisoned by its uncaring fangs, yet Jesus, King of kings, Lord of lords, true God and true man, has lent to us his authority. That authority is to be exercised in the power of the Holy Spirit, who had hovered over the waters.

So much is against us in this life. There are so many disappointments and unresolved tragedies. Evil oppresses us on every side. Our enemies (certainly ill health and accident) crowd at our door. In all these things, have we lost the courage to take hold of our authority and power? Are we continually looking over our shoulders at what Satan is doing, or is he always looking over his, wondering what we Christians are up to?

The people of the world still suffer under the serpent's bite. By God's grace, the offer to us of Christ's power and authority has not been withdrawn. Symbolically speaking, the bronze snake is nailed high on the pole, and everyone who looks at it lives. Down the centuries, through the iniquities of the human race, we have broken up, torn into shreds, and generally otherwise stained and distorted, the original, perfect reality. Jesus Christ came, full of grace and truth, to begin its restoration. What he began, he will bring to completion and fulfilment. Jesus tells us,

> "Blessed are the pure in heart, for they will see God."
> *Matthew 5:8*

If we long to see God at work, and to bring others into his healing light, we must live as Jesus lived; and we must press on into a state of holiness and discover inner purity. Is there an unfathomable secret to living on this earth as Jesus lived, or is that dream impossible, an unreasonable and unreachable intention? What is needed is effective biblical teaching and expectancy, and then we see healing of the sick. The pilgrim road to finding life and power for ministry begins not at the manger in Bethlehem but in the blood-stained dust at the foot of the cross of Jesus Christ. It is this cross that represents the high price paid by heaven, telling us both how deeply God desires our holiness and to be at one with us, and the enormous price that he was prepared to suffer and pay to make us holy.

Without the power of Pentecost, the Holy Spirit at work, there would be no possibility of effective healing ministry; but the emphasis must *first* be on the death of self and incorporation into Christ, which makes us more and more transparent to kingdom authority and power as we walk the way of obedience. If it were not for the substitutionary death of Jesus, no one could be declared in heaven to be righteous in God's sight. Without personally receiving that saving good news, we might see Jesus as an inspirational individual, but we would not know the great truth of salvation from the dominion of sin, nor the wonderful reality of new life in the body of our Lord, nor his indwelling presence, from which Christian healing ministry flows. Without the death of Jesus, none could be born again. This second birth, and the vibrant certainties of new life that spring from it, can only be ours through the death and resurrection of Jesus Christ from the dead. We are not sanctified without first being justified by God. We cannot be on the road to that sanctification without first being regenerated by the Holy Spirit. None of us is justified or regenerated without also being sanctified, and all comes only through faith in Jesus Christ.

It follows, then, that an absence of personal fellowship and communion with Jesus in our life is a very serious matter. If there is no sign of holiness in our lives, then there is no obvious and practical evidence that we have been justified or born again. This practical holiness, thankfully, will develop as we draw closer and closer to God's ideal for our lives, and as we continue to co-operate with the Holy Spirit in his target transformation of us into the image of Christ.

The provision for our divine healing all took place in the fullness of time, when Christ Jesus the Messiah came. But who today can be healed? How 'good' would a person have to be? Can we all receive it? This is a time for miracles because God chose to become incarnate in the birth of his Son, Jesus Christ, entering our damaged world in a new way, for our sake.

Amazingly, he did not choose to make his dwelling only amongst the 'best' people, the so-called 'great and good', but with anyone who would welcome him in. The Son of God did not exclude anyone from entry to his kingdom and its benefits on grounds of nation or family, or their history before they met him. On the contrary, God is 'kind to the ungrateful and the wicked':

> But love your enemies, do good to them, and lend to them without expecting to get anything back. Then your reward will be great, and you will be sons of the Most High, because he is kind to the ungrateful and wicked.
>
> *Luke 6:35*

So it is that healing grace is available for everyone. In the early days of my faith I might have found it hard to accept such astounding liberality. That God should be in a state of constant vehement anger towards the wicked seemed, to me, only right and proper; but that he should be kind towards those who defy or disobey his laws often seemed to me to be a monstrous injustice. Ha! The certainty of youth! I can find nowhere in Scripture where he gives any of us the authority to say about anyone else that they are not redeemed. We do not have his authority to describe anyone as being eternally 'lost' (that judgement is his, and his alone.) Nor does he give any wounded soul or afflicted conscience permission to tell itself that it cannot be redeemed! He came from heaven in those days not to judge us, though he undoubtedly possessed the authority to do so; he came to use his authority to save us from our sins. What does it mean to be saved? Jesus has come to rescue us from places where, in God's view, we are not meant to be. Sickness is quite definitely one of these places. He has breathed hope and salvation into our souls, and by his Holy Spirit he continues that healing work to this very day. Now Jesus is risen from the dead, living and reigning in the place of power. He is in heaven at the right hand of our heavenly Father, and pouring a continuing stream of grace upon healing grace into the church. This is not some weird delusion; it is the truth of the matter. Countless Christians have found that this is true and that the relationship with Jesus Christ as living Lord is an experienced reality, governing their lives.

So why, oh why, in the light of all this, does not everyone who comes to Christ for their healing receive it? In New Testament times, we see Jesus only too ready, willing and able to heal every sickness that was brought before him. If he is truly the same God today as he was yesterday, then *why* does it not work the same way today? Why is not Christian healing characterised by a one hundred per cent success rate in answered prayer? In theory, it should be so.

If we had the effrontery to ask that very same question of our medical profession, what would they say? In all probability, the doctors' humble answer would be only that they do not yet know enough science to guarantee complete healing every time. If we were to ask them why they could not cure AIDS and cancer with ease, they could reply that they have insufficient knowledge. The question is not often asked of the doctors. But that seems so extraordinary: we have so much expectancy in them that we visit the surgery with the slightest problem, and are overwhelmed by gratitude for everything they give us. We go to them in faith and hope, but any failure on their part is not considered to be such; it becomes one of those great imponderable things which we cannot bear to consider.

We have the foresight, though, to see a little of the way ahead in the fields of scientific research. Governments and charities pour fortune upon fortune of dedicated time and finance into greater and deeper research, so that more answers may be found. Where they are not winning they redouble their efforts.

In complete contrast, we Christians, even knowing as we do that we have Almighty God around us, shrug our shoulders at everything we do not immediately and fully understand, and write it off, straight away, to the mystery of God.

Hypothetically, if the local doctor was only able to bring healing to one in a thousand supplicants (as is sometimes the case in the ministry of prayer), then surely he would be bringing injustice both to his patients and to his science and profession. He might do well either to cease calling himself a doctor or seek re-education.

On the other hand, if a meeting in prayer takes place between a supplicant, a minister and God, without the required fruit appearing within a very short time, we fall into new depths of doubt and secret despair that one or other of them, most likely God, has let us down. The minister sometimes pays little or no heed to his own inadequacy as a deliverer of gifts, claiming that all is the responsibility of our higher authority.

We are to take authority over sickness and disease, in Jesus' name! Leaning only on the efficacy of intercessory prayer for sovereign intervention, rather than exercising delegated divine authority over sickness, can amount to evasion of our responsibility.

We may be in danger of losing sight of the power of the cross and of the authority invested in the church. We give thanks for our medical science when the glass is half full but doubt the present power of Christ to heal the sick when the glass of God's healing results appears to be half empty. Sadly enough, the glass of divine healing released may sometimes seem to contain far less than that, and looks like just dregs, a sorry sight; the fault is always entirely on our side, as the glass has been drained by our lack of expectancy of him to work miracles.

As a family, we Christians have, too often had only *partial* expectancy that our heavenly Father longs to and is able to heal all our diseases. We accept Old Testament writings that refer to him as our healer; we read, and take some comfort from, the Gospels, which are so full of healing miracles; and we admire the early and saintly giants in Acts who seemed to have very little difficulty in ministering healing. We sing about God, in our hymns and worship songs, as our healer and restorer, and yet, for the most part, much of this is empty words that are easy to say. When it comes to it, we do not really believe it!

With science, however, where knowledge is limited, we cannot bear to consider it failing us in our own circumstances of sickness. Our levels of expectancy are sky-high; while we live and remain under treatment, there is hope.

With God, whose knowledge of these things is unlimited, we tend to die away at the first hurdle, surrendering hope for despair and thoughts about our apparent distance from the Almighty. If only we look at what *is* achieved, and then persevere in pursuit of more of it, we would see miracles beyond numbering as God responds to our expecting. Through this humble expectancy and persistence in ministry, the church's delegated power for re-building bodies and minds would flourish out of all recognition. This is not to say that we have within us, by virtue only of our creation, some power of our own to re-establish into wholeness what has decayed; rather, it means that new birth brings with it an indwelling of God through his Holy Spirit, and it is that Spirit who makes real to us the will and perfect ability of Jesus to heal.

Frankly, living continuously in awe of God's healing care and concern for mankind, I sometimes find it almost incomprehensible that he should so care for us when we so often fail to honour him in these things and live by his statutes. But care he does. What blessing!

We live with increasing levels of sickness in our communities, some of it caused by lifestyle and diet, some by other causes; and we struggle to finance the care we need; many lives are ruled by disease. Yet the real story of life is that God is King! He broke into history two thousand years ago to tell us this and much more. He came to set us free from all the things that tie us down: our commitments to those unreal securities of money, possessions, houses, interest rates and the cost of living. He came to set us free from our insecurities, our hang-ups, our personality failures, our jealousies, our anger, our bitterness and all our diseases.

This is the greatest blessing of all: that he is with us and that he is concerned about each one of us. God the Holy Spirit works to draw his creation into a love relationship with him.

I confess my wondering amazement at our all-knowing, all-powerful and ever-present God. My heart seems to burst with a pure love of the living God as I pursue, and am pursued by, God in his infinite patience and love.

3

Choosing the Way

To those of us who have observed it, the healing grace of God falls like rain from heaven, gently salving and cauterising the wounds of life, be they physical, emotional or spiritual in nature. It is the work of God and, when we are open to these things, his gifts flow in levels of abundance not usually expected or seen. Little can separate us from it other than our own unbelief. None of us is too insignificant, too sinful, too ill, too old or too young to bathe in it. It fills the air with a tenderness as soft as silence and as gracious as goodness itself.

Despite all this heavenly wealth, many of the 'praise' attitudes of our larger and more lively churches involved in healing prayer seem to cover over an inability to develop, and integrate into their ministry to one another, a theology of suffering or even a love-based theology of healing. We too readily assume the harsh role of 'mechanic' or official offerer of prayer. We should be on our guard: a ministry without compassion, even if it is embedded in a sustainable theology of healing is soon a spent force.

No new ministry survives for long without these things. As potential ministers of healing we must avoid making decisions about which directions to live by, and to teach, while there is in us any unwillingness to embrace the cross of Christ and all its consequences. This is always a difficult road among a people whose demands are insatiable, whose view of God is that he should act instantly or not at all, and who tend to dismiss any divine mystery or sovereignty.

Much of Western culture-Christianity takes the view that professional success, comfort at home, good feelings, fine income levels, good physical health and a prosperity which brings overall happiness is the outworking of God's approval for the individual, and, as a result, the mark of God's friendship and presence in their lives. The inadequacy and lopsidedness of that view is self-evident. It is hardly representative of the experience of Christian life depicted and reflected in the New Testament! When things are going to plan, it is easier to feel close to the Lord. When our efforts are followed by successive bouts of failure and disaster, we soon find ourselves wondering why the rebuking word of God has descended on us from on high. All this is a very far cry from biblical reality.

Like the world around us, we tend to demand what we demand, and we do not want anything else, whether it be conceived in God's wisdom or not. If we have no present need for it, then it will not do. On the other side of the same coin, much of the modern healing ministry is infected with the world's scientific standpoint: we search diligently for the right formula for healing, the right prayers, the right attitudes, formula hunting with little allowance for the grace and the mystery of God. There is an oft-missed truth that God is not like a recipe or a photocopier, but the *source* of love and *he alone* generates his acts. We do not trigger his grace by using specific prayer or forms of service.

We forget altogether that Christ longs also to give us healthy souls, with the strength to live, to suffer and to die.

So what did I learn from my friend, as he set off along his new road to find his place in these things? How was he to begin to understand the healing ministry? What line should he take? How was he to answer the most common question of all: "Why doesn't everyone get healed?"

He found, and he passed on to me, that there are two major views of healing theology which have attained some prominence in these days. We can refer to them as the 'eschatological' and 'atonement' theories. Each one has, in their own right, justified the writing of a number of books by other authors so it may only serve here to paint a thin overview of each, rather than debate them to any great extent. The first theology, the eschatological, majors on the undoubted fact that we are living in the 'in-between' times. Jesus Christ has already visited his people as Saviour and suffering servant, but will come again from heaven as King of kings and Lord of lords. Between these two visitations there is a difference. The kingdom is already here, but not yet in fullness. If it had wholly arrived, and full healing in body, mind and spirit were to be granted to everyone on demand, then that must mean, for the Christian on being prayed for, that we would all immediately be raptured into glorified bodies and everlasting life. In other words, Christ would surely have returned because that is precisely what will happen when he does. Our healing of body, mind and spirit would be complete in an instant. But he has not yet returned. While we wait, we only see in part. God undoubtedly wishes to see all of us healed but not (necessarily) yet. The Holy Spirit comes to give us a foretaste of what is to come, not yet the full package. On this view, therefore, we must not teach and uphold that all healing is freely available; we are not to expect too much. What we do not see in miraculous cures we proclaim as the 'mystery' of God; and, truly, what would our Almighty God be without mystery? What would he be to us if we could fully understand him? So we ask. We may all ask, and we may all ask for anything. We should expect everything and expect nothing at the same time.

This theology of healing has one useful explanatory advantage in terms of pastoral care. We can say to those not yet healed, to those who feel that God may prefer others, or to those who are convinced that they have some sinful block of their own, that not everyone is supposed to be healed anyway. The feeling is that avoiding too much expectancy will reduce the level of disappointment and rejection. However, such an attitude to healing grace is counter-productive. It is this very same expectancy with which we do not wish to over-enthuse people (in case things do not work out for them) that acts as an effective 'lightning conductor', allowing kingdom healing to break through into our lives. Being advised to observe lower levels of expectancy reduces our openness to the flow of the sparkling river of grace. Avoiding expectancy, sadly, reduces the possibilities of God's work in his people. It prevents us from raising our lightning conductors but it does give us an answer to all our apparent prayer 'failings'.

On the other hand, we learned that the 'atonement' approach claims that through his wounds we are healed. He bore our sicknesses and carried our pain, and the power of them over us has been exhausted on the cross of our Lord. It is finished. The work of the cross is complete. Healing has happened already. It follows then, as it is with forgiveness and everlasting life, that all such benefits are laid up in heaven already for us and that all we have to do is ask for them. In its simplest and most naïve form, all the Christian needs is enough faith (expectancy) and all is given. This atonement theology of healing increases dramatically our wonder at the work of God on the cross, but tends to reduce in our minds any sense of his present mystery. It suggests that as long as we can grasp the fullness of Calvary we can come close to holding in our minds the fullness of God's gifts to us. Enough faith and we are healed.

Having debated this view at some length, we at least agreed that, especially in the light of Calvary, God most certainly has the right to be trusted, to be believed in what he says, and to see us entirely depend on his love. In pastoral terms, such a line of thought has the weighty advantage of lifting both the minister's and the supplicant's expectancy, raising even higher into heaven our 'lightning conductors'. Miracles follow, and judging from our experience of healing meetings and witness testimonies, many more than emerge from the first theological standpoint discussed here.

The disadvantage we found with the atonement theology is that the unhealed may be left either in a state of condemnation for lack of faith, or in resentment and anger at having been hoodwinked into a temporary state of emotional overdrive, carried away by the elation or atmosphere of the moment. There is often a feeling of rejection by God, and the supplicant is left with only one possible way forward into healing, and that is by their own efforts—by working harder at their own faith—which can be a most ungracious and ungodly principle.

Faith very occasionally evaporates altogether, though a more common reaction would be one of a feeling of being rejected by God for lack of it.

The only valid question has to be: are people being healed? Both theologies, it would seem to me, serve little purpose in this world unless they fall out of the tips of our fingers with the compassionate love and power of God himself. Otherwise, such debates may only serve as a thin soup for the nourishment of other theologians—unless, of course, we set out to put the theories into practice. But while the timid wonder, the wise men ask.

Behind these theories is the beating heart and the enquiring mind of those who know that somehow there has to be more than there is, much more. There is a danger that our leaders may choose and develop their theology with their focus on pastoral inferences. Such cares as these are mostly misdirected, as the unhealed are left with feelings of rejection either way. We have already noticed that whilst we accept that medical approaches can sometimes fail, or be inconclusive and unsatisfactory from the sufferer's perspective, we tend to accept those shortcomings much more easily than 'failures' of Christian healing ministry. Such a common and illogical position leaves us wide open to feelings of rejection, and the minister's theology will have little or no bearing on that fact. However Christian healing is taught among the people, faith is rarely lost in the face of unanswered prayer and, when it is, it may well have been a faith that was not worth the keeping. While I wait for my own healing, I know there is a sun even when it is behind the clouds; I know that there is love in the world, even on those days that I do not feel it; and I know that there is a God, even when he appears to be silent.

The truth at ground level is that we know that he has placed everything under the feet of Jesus and yet we do not see everything behaving as if it were so. We know that Jesus has been given authority over all things but, so far, not everything, and certainly not our illnesses of body and mind, conduct themselves as if under holy instruction. Some do, and for that we praise him. Some do not and we will praise him, whilst wondering why things are not working out as they should.

The theologian addressing Christian healing is pressed into choosing between the eschatological and the atonement view so that he might answer the question which is uppermost in the minds of many: why is not every sickness and disease subject to him in reality? Why is not everyone healed?

Which of these two theologies is more correct? Which view should we associate ourselves with? Which stand should we take? What is popular is not always right, and what is right is not always popular.

It was at this point in our joint venture that my priestly mentor and I parted company, hardly for any spiritual reason but because of his promotion within the ranks of the Anglican Church and the consequent in-rushing of other demands on his life. It was for me, then, to go on alone, with humility, in a third direction. Standing at this fork in the road, I became the pilgrim minister, driven on by the Holy Spirit into the things of God, asking only of myself and of my Lord: 'For the sake of your beloved ones, how can I help to see more of that which was evil coming into holy submission? How do I do better battle for the oppressed? How do I see more under his feet? If I had more grace, more wisdom, more power and more submissiveness to God's authority, how much more can I do? How much, in this present world, are we supposed to see under his feet?'

This pilgrim servant healer soon became much less concerned as to the whys and wherefores of failure but with the optimism and hope of more. Out of this third walk grew a third theology of healing. Instead of spending time wondering why certain individuals do not appear to be healed, one searches instead to be a greater channel of service oneself. This way claims that healing flows from the foot of the cross of Christ; that miracles happen by God's grace when the river of his will meets with our expectancy.

When there is sufficient simple, child-like faith expectancy, persistence and humility, Jesus wills to see everyone healed who asks him —everyone. He has demonstrated our heavenly Father's will in these things in his own earthly ministry, and God does not change. Healing should happen. There are no sins, no blockages, no hang-ups and no lack of religious fervour that can limit his love (though unforgiveness, perhaps a wound suffered at the hand of another, can prevent us from receiving from him.) Our ability to receive the healing power of God is dependent on our resistance to doubt. Whenever two or three are gathered together in his name, it should happen. Wherever God finds expectancy larger than a mustard seed, it should happen. Whenever the body of Christ is in agreement in his name, it should happen. Wherever the kingdom of God is near, it should happen. And this remains the mystery: it does not always work the way it should. There are times when heaven seems to fall silent.

The eschatological view of healing dismisses all these apparently unanswered prayers as being the mystery of God, and in that dismissal we ministers will cease to become pilgrims, locking ourselves into a lazy-minded state of lack of understanding, through submission to the status quo, which stifles growth. We say that we do our part by offering to pray, and the rest is all between the supplicant and God.

The atonement theory on its own, when faced with the absence of a sought-after miracle, can only suggest some blame in the supplicant for lack of faith, thus blocking any further possibilities for growth in any other area than in the sufferer himself.

Either way, and here is the fault line in both theologies, the minister is excused from any responsibility. We may debate at length the emotional state or the spiritual receptiveness of the sufferer. We may argue the virtues of the eschatological and atonement theologies of healing. Is it God's will to demonstrate his Fatherhood or not? Does he love to give us a foretaste of heaven to come?

Like others on this pilgrimage road, I am learning never to be disappointed, but always to praise. I deeply suspect that it must hurt our Father's tender love when we contend with his Holy Spirit, and each other, because of apparent shortcomings in his dealings with us, in ways we do not at first understand —as if it was someone else who chose our inheritance for us; as if he is not Love; and as if what he chooses to allow could conceivably be something less than the very best and most loving that the light of his eternal love has to shower on us.

I do not necessarily find a position of unbroken

peacefulness and complete inner harmony over all these things. The variety of tensions between the various theologies and philosophies within the healing ministry is not like a softly cushioned easy chair in which to relax in some afternoon meditation pose. Rather, the healing ministry of the Christian church is a fort in enemy country, and the forces that oppose us are most cunning, and adept at surprise assault. However, there can be nothing for us to fear. Our ministries and our particular theological interpretations are not like military or political positions, for us to hold on to at all costs; rather, we are in a place in which we are kept safely, by grace, as long as, in the moment of attack, we fix our eyes on Jesus, the author and perfecter of our faith, remaining faithful to his precious word. In the lull between the battles, we do well to step tentatively out of our fortresses onto the pilgrimage road, honestly and humbly clasping our ignorance in our hands, seeking not so much how we might understand all the unanswered questions, but how we might, as ministers of his grace, serve our Lord more faithfully tomorrow than yesterday. The question before us is not one whose answer we might use to justify 'failures' in ministry.

Of course we may finish up anywhere. This is the risk of the pilgrim way. We may even end our days having gone round in a circle, back into those earliest of ministry times, when the church simply expected these things to happen. So how may we look simply at a more positive way forward into healing? What plain ideas leave open the possibility of setting us on the road to even greater effectiveness in healing ministry?

Jesus healed of all their diseases all those who asked him, and all healing was full and was given without delay.

He claimed that he did not do or say anything unless God the Father was doing it. We may conclude that it is God's will to see everyone healed today. We may try to justify our lack of healing with other ideas. The kind of suffering sometimes referred to in the Bible as being of value in character building is not a function of illness but of persecution. Suffering that comes from disease is not the will of God. Its continuing existence through ill health cannot be used to justify any delay in divine healing. Remember that Jesus would not even wait for the Sabbath to finish, the healing of the sick was so urgent. To Calvary's cross Christ took all our sicknesses and there he bore all our diseases. By his wounds we are healed. The treasure chest of healing grace is opened for us in heaven. Expectancy, persistence and humility work together as the components of the lightning conductor that earths heaven's grace in healing and wholeness. Although the expectancy of the minister and supplicant are of great value, the way of openness to receiving grace is through corporate expectancy of the body gathered. There is no sin, wound, demon, bondage or any other blockage (other than doubt) that can hinder the healing of the sick by means of the power that comes from God. Having stated all that, not everyone is healed. The prime, and insufficiently explored, reason for this apparent lack of answered prayer lies in the fact that Jesus has entrusted his healing ministry to the church. Had he kept it for himself, and answered prayer only by the route of direct sovereign intervention, the ministry would 'work' perfectly every time. So, as we have been given delegated responsibility for it, how should the church be exercising this healing ministry to best effect? By exercising her authority! Jesus Christ has been given authority over all things, including sickness, and has passed on that authority to his disciples. He has two ways of answering prayer: sovereignly, and through his people. It is the second of these that seems to be his preferred route, and it is opened up not by intercessory prayer requesting sovereign action but by the church herself, as she commands healing and dismisses evil with the authority she has been given to do so. The use of such authority in love is powerful and effective. The flow of the power of God always follows his given authority, but only where that authority is deeply understood by the disciple and is thoroughly maintained by that disciple in the context of his or her own sonship. God is willing and powerful to heal, so we need to consider three things: firstly, we must think of the **corporate expectancy of the gathered body** rather than the 'faith shortfall' in the supplicant; secondly, those who minister need to ensure that we are **exercising our authority in the deepest compassion**; and, thirdly, only after the possibilities of the first two have been exhausted, may we in our frail human thinking, ascribe any continued delay in healing to the mystery of God. This is the way of responsibility.

4

A Question of Faith

Teaching this ever-flowing river of healing grace is a source of pure delight to me, but one question about my own blindness is constantly recurring:

"Why, then, haven't you been healed?"

I have never taken such remarks as being either personal or critical of the teaching that we have a God who renews and heals. It is an honest enough statement of unknowing, verging on sincere doubt, that finds itself more comfortable in another and more popular guise. Why does God allow tragedy to strike us down and, in the absence of any understandable reply, why does he not answer our every prayer cried out of the common nightmare of our disasters?

Indeed we do have a responsibility, towards our fellow Christian family members, to attempt to allay their fears. Apparent lack of divine reply is not always an easy thing to explain. If we are searching for a particular solution concerning a particular person we may never find it —

there is no cover-all diagnosis, no easy answer for gifts not given to a particular individual, though sometimes when ministry is given the Holy Spirit graciously reveals barriers to receiving which can be dealt with.

Jesus healed everyone who asked him, and told us that he only did what he saw the Father doing. We can only assume, then, that it is God's certain will that all who come to him should be healed. And one thing is for sure —he does not love any one of us any less than another. So why does any one individual appear to miss out? We might begin to glimpse a better understanding of this Christian quandary if we ask a slightly different question: if everyone who asks is offered healing by our Lord, then why is it that some receive more effectively than others? In my own case, I am, in these days and at my age, a little uncertain about the emotional change that would be involved in the restoration of my sight. I have been blind for a number of years and lead a successful life as a blind person. I can, in short, work it the way it is, and I do not suffer over it in any way. It is simply not a problem to me. To jump sideways into a sighted world seems to me to be a culture-change fraught with difficulties that I might not handle very well. It would be very like a Frenchman saying to an Italian, 'Perhaps you would like to be French?' —and implying that he would be far better off in the process!

However, while we continue to focus on our 'failures', we will fail even more; whereas, when we direct our energies to advancing our 'success', we see more and greater miracles than ever before. We should at least begin by examining the water-table of faith expectancy in the body of Christ. If we judge its level by the shortage of healing of illnesses in the church today, we might conclude that it is very low, the ground is very dry, and that our collective faith expectancy of God is smaller than a mustard seed.

> Then the disciples came to Jesus in private and asked, "Why couldn't we drive it out?"
> He replied, "Because you have so little faith. I tell you the truth, if you have faith as small as a mustard seed, you can say to this mountain, 'Move from here to there' and it will move. Nothing will be impossible for you."
>
> *Matthew 17:19–20*

In truth, so much healing is longed for and yet is unrealisable —the major cause of such impossibility being the shrinking of mustard seeds. The smaller they become the less we expect, and the less we expect the more our mustard seed shrinks.

The working life of any minister of God's healing grace is, to a greater or lesser extent in each one of us, a matter of tension between two great facts. One of them is the word of God, and the other is our experience of filled and unfulfilled promises in the High Street of life. Then there are the forces of Satan, desperately concerned with denying to us the full force of Calvary that ripped apart the temple curtain. The demonic foe that opposes the work of God seeks to whisper in our ear, 'This cannot be possible!'

I find the Scriptures to be clear: Jesus, in his reflecting of the Father's love, wants to and will provide all the necessary power to heal everyone who asks him for that divine grace and favour. "Don't be afraid," he says, "just believe." (See Mark 5:36). And, "Do not be afraid, little flock, for your Father has been pleased to give you the kingdom" (Luke 12:32).

On the other hand, cures do not always happen. In common with many others of God's children, we ask in faith, and situations of illness remain. When they do, we retreat, in great spiritual bewilderment, into a whole mêlée of often unscriptural medieval philosophies about God's will, in order to defend to ourselves God's apparent inaction. The underlying wrong belief, often stated in the frustration of being faced, for example, with the medically incurable, is that God wills sickness onto his people, for some mysterious ends of his own. This does not accurately portray the God of love.

The more enlightened ones, more aware that God is love, justify their lack of receiving healing by proclaiming that, while God did not make the illness occur, he is withholding healing for his own purposes. This twisted logic is exactly the same as the false understanding that God gives disease; it merely *sounds* like a deeper piece of theology. Such beliefs remain as offensive and dirty stains on the faith of the church. The greatest act of sacrifice, the death of the Son of God himself, did not bring death to his people but abundant life. By his wounds we are healed, not diseased. He came that we might have life, and have it in abundance, and not to prolong the agonies of this world. He came not to condemn us but to save us from our sins.

If we appear to fail in our prayers for a relatively minor complaint then we shrug our shoulders and ponder it no more. However, if a dear friend or a spouse is taken from us through some life threatening disease, and we have been so sure that God was about to heal them, our faith becomes totally devastated. This abrupt downward turn in our trust in God is not only a coming together of all our tragic sentiments of grief, but finds its echo in the same and strangest feeling that Jesus himself experienced in the darkness on Calvary: "Eloi, Eloi, lama sabachthani?"—which means, "My God, my God, why have you forsaken me?"

So many of us, holding tightly onto our breaking and grieving hearts, and anaesthetizing our minds against the tension of scriptural truth versus factual circumstance, begin to turn away. We leave, at any rate for the time being, the hope that God heals, justifying our retreat by denying that calling, given to every Christian, to be involved in the healing of the wounded on the battleground of life on this earth. Tragically, we begin to lose trust when we need it most.

Every time such prayers appear not to be answered, we allow our faith (expectancy) levels to drop and, once they have become smaller than a mustard seed, we see miracles no longer. Of course we continue to offer prayer out of love and Christian duty, but that is all our ministry becomes —a ministry of prayer. What was a reliable engine may now only be running on vapour! There is, however, another road to follow. We might just as easily take the line, as would our medical professionals, that we have failed only because we do not, as yet, know enough. We might come out of such prayer failures with an even greater determination to press further and further into the things of heaven, to find new fields of love and holy power to explore and fruits to bring to God's struggling people.

This is not the easiest route. How much easier it would be to shrug our shoulders and be dismissive of God's yearning heart! The golden nugget of that simple, child-like trust in him, to which Jesus always responds so readily, seems harder to grasp as the centuries pass. In these days we may all have been affected, much more than we realise, by the steady influence of this age's materialistic and scientific perspective. Rejecting all else in the end, we are inclined to believe only the things that we can understand or that our professionals can explain to us. Our plans and efforts for the extension of Christ's kingdom are threatened by this invasion of the church by the scientific world view. Anti-supernatural materialism (by which we mean a virtual denial that anything other than the material exists) has infected the thinking of many Christians. It leads to a watery spiritual life and a lack of spiritual vision and vitality. A secularised church can never have the focus to evangelise the world. This is mainly because science, in most of the industrialised world and in many of our church pews, is held up by the majority, quite falsely, to be something of a god in its own right, the fountain of all knowledge and help in time of trouble. We give full credence to the laws of science, but many of us reject the laws and gifts of God, our Creator and sustainer, with whom nothing is impossible.

Some other gifts of God are much easier to understand than healing miracles. We are able to trust that God will bring us peace in this life because we could almost see how to work it into that state by ourselves, given enough time, money, patience and love, and sufficient political will and skill. But we find it difficult to believe that God would heal the sick, simply because we cannot understand how he could possibly do it. His methods are often far from the accepted scientific route, leaving us with no good explanation against which we might judge the potential of the healer. All we are left with is yet more scepticism and unbelief, easily the most powerful suppressants of miracle working.

An eight-year-old boy with big round eyes sat quite quietly on his mother's knee, his attention glued to the goings-on at his first visit to a church. He had a weakness, a hole in the heart, for which he was on the point of having an operation, and his mother was requesting prayer from us for the forthcoming trial. Prayers for healing were offered and answered: the idea of an operation was later abandoned by the hospital consultant as being unnecessary. The hole was healed.

Another lady came, within a few hours of this thrilling news, to ask Jesus Christ for healing, having lost, it seemed to her, her fight against cancer which had continued for some months, despite the able support of her medical team. After much devoted prayer in her home congregation she died, leaving behind her a devastated family and a church's corporate faith feeling as though it had been run over by a steamroller.

One and not the other! Can we understand these things? Shall we doubt the power of healing prayer because we see such 'failures' or shall we re-group, re-train, re-examine our own ministry and fight on? Unhappily, God's people do not always believe in God's power in these areas, and perhaps we are tempted to feel that we should not be expected to, when faced with some of the evidence before our eyes. However, we must admit that it is sheer arrogance on our part to doubt a word or a promise from God simply because we do not understand it. That is reducing our concept of God to the level of our own poor human minds.

Here we are, though, living in a society that readily seeks to place blame wherever it can for things gone amiss. Our expectancy of every area of Government—education, health, law and order, the whole economic area—is of a mountainous proportion. Whenever we feel that our expectancies are cheated, we demand the apportionment of blame and the exacting of penalty. This blame 'need' is, no doubt, one of the planks in our Western cultural desire for revenge, for exacting payment for apparent wrongdoing. This social flavour presents us with a number of difficulties which are unresolvable to the mind that does not also seek the deeper things of God.

As an example of our subconscious need to point the finger, when healing prayer appears to fall on deaf ears in the heavenly realms, we begin to wonder if the fault could lie with the minister, with the supplicant or with God, whose word clearly announces his willingness and power to heal. Perhaps the minister is not sufficiently holy to be a clean channel for God's gifts? We might be critical of his style; we might 'prefer' other types of ministry; we might spend years in search of a minister through whom God is prepared to work the particular miracle we seek. Perhaps the supplicant did not, at the time of praying, have the right attitude of heart to allow the incoming grace to take root? Perhaps there are as yet unplumbed depths of inner hurt that God wishes to heal first? Was there some sin or lowliness of estate too vast for God to step across?

All these questions are openly asked and rarely answered by a healing ministry which is happy to accept its own limitations. We have to accept that healing is not always received —but how negative! Which is easier to say: "I don't know", or, "I'll go and find out!"? Which is easier to say: "It's all part of the mystery of God", or, "I will spend my life, if that's what it needs, waiting on the mountain for his revelation about these things!" Which is easier to say: "Your sins are forgiven", or, "Get up and walk!"?

Let us begin by commenting on our understanding of the word of God. At least we might find that this path of enquiry is the more fruitful exercise —such pressing down through the surface sand of the Scriptures to find the wells of living water causes the sparks of faith to fly. We cannot acquire a good understanding of Scripture, the basis of any genuine ministry, by the use of our intellect alone. The word of God is the instructing power of the revelation of our infinite God in this finite world. Holding it to be revelation, our first duty when approaching it is to begin in prayer, entreating our Lord to grant us, out of his great mercy, the true understanding of his word. We will, after all, never find a better interpreter of the word of God than the Author himself. As he has said,

> "It is written in the Prophets: 'They will all be taught by God.' Everyone who listens to the Father and learns from him comes to me."
>
> *John 6:45*

We need the Holy Spirit to aid us in understanding the word and its application as we seek to learn more from the Scriptures about healing. Whether we think of ourselves as standing on Mount Carmel with Elijah, leaning on the promises of God and waiting for the fire to fall or, like Job, wrestle with the details of awful private circumstance in the face of the God of love, it is here in our wrestling that the sparks are ignited, the flames of faith leap higher, and our faith itself faces the prospect of its own revival, again and again.

If falling deeper into the enfolding word of God is

beneficial to the soul and to our understanding of God and his ways, then what of our need to apportion fault, and discover a reason for the apparent failure of what seems at the time to be unanswered prayer? The main answer, quite simply, lies in the fact that our Lord has delegated the healing ministry to the church. Rather than keeping the dispensing of this gift away from his imperfect children, look at the terrifying risks that God has taken with believers. In considering this divine generosity of heart, we do not need to explain or modify, but simply revel in his unremitting love towards mankind. He is relying on sinful and ignorant human beings to do the work he has given them to do, empowered by his Holy Spirit!

The 'eschatological' theological approach to divine healing is inclined to put all our unanswered prayers into two pigeon holes: either the supplicant's faith is somehow lacking, or everything we do not understand is simply written off as being the mystery of God.

The 'atonement' theory, on the other hand, leaving little or no room for this mystery tends to ascribe all our lack of success at the door of the supplicant. Whatever has gone wrong, they and they alone must sort themselves out. In neither mainstream of thought does the minister take any responsibility at all for outcomes.

But had Christ kept this ministry for himself, had he been the sole party involved in the healing of sickness, had the ministry been completely free of all sin, then we would have perfection indeed! 'It' would work every time!

What must our attitude be in the church about 'success' and 'failure' when it comes to the measure of answered prayer for healing? Certainly, lack of success among our scientists simply drives them on to understand more in the hope of greater achievement; it does not make them surrender, with their hands in the air, to the current state of things.

So where do we start our research? What sin, what horrific stain in the church constricts the flow of grace? What evil still has the power to form a solid wall between heaven and earth? Whatever is it that could be lying, almost unnoticed, in the body of Christ and restrict the flow of the river of God in this way?

The great *blocking* sin of the church of the present day is our general unbelief in the work of the Holy Spirit; our lack of trusting expectancy that he will act. It is not God who limits his gifts but our shortfall in expectation that restricts our receiving the miraculous. What sometimes passes for Christian faith is too enfeebled. Common enough is a vague idea that God is some sort of general force for good, and even that he is the source of any goodness in action that springs up from time to time in human beings. True as that is, much too uncommon is the kind of relationship with God that is characterised by the trusting look on the face of an adoring child, waiting with complete assurance of expectancy at the Father's knee. It is this latter state that mixes so easily with the incoming flow of grace to cause a miracle to happen.

So are we to blame the minister or the supplicant for lack of anointing, or for weakness of faith and spiritual skill? Or shall we make such a judgement over some poor suffering soul —that they do not believe strongly enough in God? By no means, for none of this reflects the love and healing design of the God we call Almighty! Blaming and judging invites condemnation; moreover, some blaming for lack of faith can unwittingly introduce the false philosophy of 'mind over matter'. We must always bear in mind that God can and does heal those who have not yet come to faith, and orthodox believing is not a sort of hurdle that the supplicant needs to jump before effective ministry is given and received. There is an important link between healing and evangelism, but this is not a matter of imposing pre-conditions for healing. The kind of faith that is vitally significant, though, is **corporate expectancy**. It is that utter confidence in God that he will beneficially answer our prayers, a confidence that needs to be manifested in a praising, believing body, which opens up the faulty situations to his grace.

Thank God that we should have to be expectant; but we should not expect to have to have all the expectancy. No one individual, supplicant or minister, need carry the burden, or the guilt, of having to believe well enough for a miracle.

In matters of miracle working, belief and unbelief is measured in heaven on a corporate basis, however large or small the body at prayer on any specific occasion might be. The value of this precious dispensation can be seen in the rise and fall of individual expectancy toward God, that he will be present in power to heal the sick. We all have measures of faith (by which we mean, in this context, expectancy). Any as yet unhealed areas within the minister might reduce his expectancy for God to move in that same place in others. On the other hand, where an individual minister has received dramatic divine healing in, let us say, his lungs, then he may well have heightened faith to add into the proceedings unfolding before him in similar areas of need.

For by the grace given me I say to every one of you:
Do not think of yourself more highly than you ought,

but rather think of yourself with sober judgment, in accordance with the measure of faith God has given you.

Just as each of us has one body with many members, and these members do not all have the same function, so in Christ we who are many form one body, and each member belongs to all the others.

Romans 12:3–4

In Christ, we who are many form one body. Clearly, the individual expectancies of the minister, the supplicant and the surrounding body are seen in heaven as being one body at prayer. As this is the case, no specific individual need feel that they have fallen short in any way. Let there be no sense of condemnation! We are a body struggling together in the darkness of a fallen world, crying '*Abba*, Father!' out of its nightmare.

It is a truth that a hundred musical instruments all perfectly tuned to the same fork are automatically tuned to each other. They are a beautiful sound that attracts the ear of the listener because of their being tuned, not to one another, but to another leading note to which they must individually submit.

Corporate expectancy within the gathered body cannot be achieved by any artificial device at the moment of its being needed. A hundred worshippers meeting together are nearer to each other in heart, as each of them looks to Christ, than they could possibly be if they turned their eyes away from God and began to strive for greater expectancy out of duty to their leadership or some organisational imperative.

The body becomes stronger as, together, its members

become more expectant. The whole church of God gains when the members together begin to expect a better and a higher quality of life with God, his will is done, and the sick are healed.

Some illnesses require of us a greater lifting of expectancy than others, and there may be unbelief about things miraculous within the body. When we take the corporate approach, God allows us the greatest hope of succeeding and we please him more. How gracious of him to allow it to be this way!

As the gathered body, in any one place at any one time, we must have faith expectancy that God will keep his promises to us. We need to seek him first, and all these things will be given to us. This is the faith that uproots trees, moves mountains, calms the sea, extinguishes fire, heals the sick and raises the dead. Have faith!

5

Authority and Sonship

Reading between the throw-away lines of spiritual chatter, there is a widespread belief abroad in the body of Christ that God has the ability to heal but seems not inclined to do so any more —or not very often. Even when he does heal, his working is often 'explained away' as being 'mind over matter' or as something that might have been about to happen anyway. Such negative expectancy toward God does not usually flow from intellectual reflection or the study of Scripture and church history, but stems rather from a simple and straightforward lack of teaching on, and experience of, the supernatural.

Cessationists would claim that such gifts are now of no further use to God, as perfection has come to us in the form of the gift of the whole canon of Scripture; but perfection will only come when we can see him face to face, at the return of Christ himself. In the intervening times we live in now, we can only follow with obedience the way that God works his will in the world.

Whilst the eschatological theology that we have already discussed leaves most of our disappointments to the mystery of God in these in-between times, and the atonement discourse tends to leave the supplicant and his faith levels at fault, there is another argument offered here for consideration. Perhaps there is another reason for so much unanswered ministry: maybe the church has mislaid most of her God-given power because she has abdicated her responsibilities for the healing of the sick. She has surrendered her authority over illness.

We need to see here that there are two ways in which healing grace flows into our world: by sovereign interjection, and through the authority of the disciples of Christ. We know that God can, and does, move sovereignly to meet people's needs in answer to prayer, but this does not seem to be the preferred route. What looks from the human perspective like the great risk God takes is that he has placed his ministry into the hands of Christians, his authority and power into the hands of the church, and, by this grace, accomplishes the majority of his works that way. Only the minority of healing miracles occur through direct, sovereign action. If we rely on the lesser used route, as we most usually do, we will see the smaller amount of traffic. We will witness fewer results.

Here is the reason both for my consternation at the great amount of suffering and rejection from seemingly unanswered prayer, and for my great expectation and hope in the potential: our habit is to offer healing prayer to Jesus, in the presence of the supplicant, and thereby to call for direct divine intervention out of heaven —seemingly the less preferred route. No wonder only a minority of those we pray for gain the kingdom benefits!

In putting everything in creation under the authority of

his only begotten Son, Jesus Christ, God has left nothing, no clinging sin or disease, that is not subject to that authority. And yet not everything behaves that way. Until we arrive in such a blissful world where all is indeed under direct divine control, this licence to exercise authority on behalf of Christ has been given to the church to share in his ministry.

His intention in making us, the church, his body, imparting his mind and his Spirit, is that now, through our lives and our ministries to one another, the grace of God should be made widely known to all the rulers and authorities in the heavenly places. What so readily flows in is to overflow. The authority that comes from God is to be applied, through us, to situations of sickness and sin. The church does, indeed, possess this authorisation: to inform all dark powers, including our sin and sicknesses, that the lordship of Jesus applies over everything, including our bodies, even when they are under attack. We are to declare the victory of Jesus over all, for he is the Lord who says,

> "All authority in heaven and on earth has been given to me."
>
> *Matthew 28:18b*

Much earlier, the disciples had begun to learn of his authority:

> He called his twelve disciples to him and gave them authority to drive out evil spirits and to heal every disease and sickness.
>
> *Matthew 10:1*

So we should place far less emphasis, in our own lives, on telling God what enormous problems we have, and spend more of our time telling our problems what a powerful God we have!

In Matthew chapter nine, we read of Jesus going through all the towns and villages, teaching in synagogues, preaching the good news of the kingdom and healing every disease and sickness that the people brought to him. In the wake of that campaign, he calls his twelve disciples to him and gives them authority to drive out evil spirits and to heal every disease and sickness. Notice that he does not instruct them to pray that God might perhaps do it for them, he gives them the authority to do it for themselves. As they went about their daily business, they were to preach this message: that 'the kingdom of heaven is near'. They were to heal the sick, raise the dead, cleanse those who had leprosy and drive out demons. Freely they had received, freely they were to give. (See Matthew 10:7.)

One of many examples of the amazing authority that was being delegated to disciples is this:

Some men brought to him a paralytic, lying on a mat. When Jesus saw their faith, he said to the paralytic, "Take heart, son; your sins are forgiven."

"...But so that you may know that the Son of Man has authority on earth to forgive sins...." Then he said to the paralytic, "Get up, take your mat and go home." And the man got up and went home.

When the crowd saw this, they were filled with awe; and they praised God, who had given such authority to men.

Matthew 9:2,6–8

The earliest disciples were to exercise this authority to full effect. They had learned of their new, delegated authority by being with, and no doubt carefully watching, our Lord himself.

These things create two assumptions. The first is that the kingdom is a place of authority, passed down from the Godhead, through Jesus Christ, and given to we disciples. The second is that power, the power to change things, will follow out of heaven the exercise of that authority.

How have I come to this conclusion —that the church has authority from God to stamp on sickness, and to stamp it out? What, we may ask, is this kind of prayer that stamps out evil?

Our usual form of prayer is to ask God to descend from heaven and fulfil the supplicant's needs and desires, working in the mind and body for healing. The needy one speaks to the minister, and then the minister speaks to God on their behalf, requesting grace to be bestowed. This style flows directly from the Old Testament character of priesthood, in which a priest was someone who came to God on behalf of the people, and came to the people on behalf of God.

This is intercession, not ministry. We intercede for the supplicant standing in front of us, we do not minister Christ's healing grace to them as we were all instructed and authorized to do, in the great commission.

This way is the one we have already characterised as not being, since the coming of Jesus Christ, God's preferred way of working. In the new covenant, we who are many form one body. In prayer, we are looked down upon from heaven as a corporate entity.

Jesus, who must be our example in all these things, seems never to have interceded (directly and specifically) immediately in advance of healing anyone —with one exception, his dead friend Lazarus. (Though raising the dead is something different from what we usually term healing.) Even that prayer was only for the teaching benefit of the onlookers. The method preferred in heaven is for the minister to take authority over the supplicant's illness and command healing in Jesus' name. An example of the authoritative exercise of delegated power would be: "Take up your mat and go home!"

Far and away the most fruitful kind of healing ministry is for the Christian to take hold of his God-given kingdom authority in Jesus Christ, and speak to illness of all kinds, dismissing it, as Jesus himself has taught us to do by his own example. The best context for this is one of corporate expectancy. The proper use of kingdom authority releases, through the body of Christ, the power to heal, and the Holy Spirit acts in accordance with the divine promises.

Worryingly, taking direct authority over sickness for the first time leaves us wide open to the danger of being reduced in front of our fellows and the flock. The egg-on-face risk here is very considerable.

To some who have been interceding for years, this way of ministering may take a little while to become the natural method of choice. There will be a desire to first weigh up carefully this different approach in the light of the Scriptures, to observe others who employ it, maybe putting it to the leadership, taking time for reflection, and then quietly testing out the idea in private. As we try to deal with our apprehensions, we are reminded of the embarrassing story of Peter climbing out of the boat. He begins his attempt with holy bravado, only to sink back into the waters of his panic. (See Matthew 14.) It was

AUTHORITY AND SONSHIP

only when Peter stepped out in obedience and followed Jesus rather than his natural fears and view of the circumstances that he discovered God can do the seemingly impossible!

Peter's story of walking on the water may raise up familiar feelings. We may, in the past, have had a vision of making a mark for God, and ardour for his kingdom encouraged us to take bold strides for him. Then, perhaps, we lost our nerve and the initiative failed. Once bitten, twice shy! The experience of feeling idiotic makes us become tentative, and perhaps a little less enthusiastic about the kingdom. We begin to lose that youthful eagerness for doing anything that our Lord may want us to do. We are in danger of cooling off. We are more attracted to the idea of becoming formal. Our Christianity begins to lose its sense of adventure. It is, after all, never safe outside the boat, but:

> It is not up in heaven, so that you have to ask, "Who will ascend into heaven to get it and proclaim it to us so that we may obey it?" Nor is it beyond the sea, so that you have to ask, "Who will cross the sea to get it and proclaim it to us so that we may obey it?" No, the word is very near you; it is in your mouth and in your heart so that you may obey it.
>
> *Deuteronomy 30:12–14*

The possibility of directly addressing sickness with God-given authority infects us with fear of criticism —that we might seem, somehow, to be working out of, and claiming, glory and power for ourselves. This fear is the food of Satan: it frightens us away from God's true intention in delegating healing authority to his church and it prevents us from realising the power of the cross and demonstrating it by healing the sick in numbers that cannot be ignored.

In passing, we note, because it sometimes arises in the course of healing ministry, that those who exercise a ministry of deliverance from the presence or effects of evil spirits find it utterly appropriate to address them directly. Seldom, though, will most of us, for whatever reasons, use the same direct method of address, as Jesus did, to the demonic entities. There are, in most Christian denominations and fellowships, precautionary rules about who should carry out that kind of ministry, and under what circumstances, and proper, scriptural safeguards need to be observed. It is often thought that deliverance ministry should remain within the sphere of specialists, appointed and ordained by the church for the purpose. However, in order to receive and maintain such a direct ministry in the church, the authority received from God is a prerequisite. The impartation of that authority needs to be fully understood by all; the church hierarchy, for its part, needs to acknowledge and recognise the anointing.

In a sense, we can see ourselves as having been given a ministerial toolbox which contains a set of tools, not a telephone! When Jesus told the disciples to go and heal the sick, he would not have expected them to keep asking whether that was what he really wanted in each case. They had the delegated authority, so they were to go out and do the job! We are called to be his agents and 'engineers' in the world, not sales consultants who need to keep checking with head office about every minor detail of the given task! That is not to say we are 'independent' operators; on the contrary, we are always to keep in step with the Spirit and in ongoing prayer communion with the Lord. The point is simply that too many Christians are very passive indeed about this whole area, and have not yet learnt to actually DO what disciples have been instructed to get out and do! We can be trained by the church, tooled up, taught and empowered by the living God, and commissioned by Jesus to follow him in all things and do the things he did —and more, because his Spirit given at Pentecost meant that healing and proclamation of the gospel alike could now go out worldwide. When we received Jesus as Saviour and Lord, we were welcomed out of our pigsties and turned into trusted and competent sons; we were not commissioned to be 'armchair Christians' but his active agents in the world!

These words about authority should touch much more than our ministry to illness of the body. If only we would allow them to sink deep into our being! If only we would refuse and reject forbidding thoughts and feelings, and believe that *even to us* this healing grace is given, we shall indeed find rest and peace about these things.

It is in that rest that we will climb, rising up on eagles' wings. Those who cannot find peace in the knowledge of our own God-given authority will not be able to climb, they will be too busy adjusting and readjusting their own concerns to have the breath or the strength to spare for such holy activity.

The exercise of such authority, given by God, according to the scriptural commands, under the precious anointing, in the power of the Holy Spirit, is a source of considerable joy to those who participate in it. This joy of the Lord is our strength, and the saints of old were full of it. Often faced with extremely adverse, oppressive circumstances, joy and love breathed out of them nonetheless, leaving those around them feeling that they must have some enormously blessed secret to impart to them. They did! As it must have been for so many of them, the acceptance of responsibility, and being treated as being responsible, brings a joy to us that is nothing frothy: this is not a question of human jollity. This peace and joy in the course of exercising delegated authority is simply the fall-out of our perfect assent and obedience to God's will, and it grows, because the soul delights itself in God himself.

Of course, taking such authority places the minister at enormous risk if nothing should happen. He stands to lose face before the people, and before those near him, for whose spiritual life he cares and feels responsible. But take heart! God is there, waiting for us on the edge of our risk-taking, because it is there that we are exercising the greatest trust and the utmost reliance on him.

In another sense, such risks cannot be lightly undertaken. For the sake of those we minister to, and for the sake of the upholding of the name of Jesus in due reverence, we need to ensure that we are not simply sounding off like a clanging cymbal. It is easy to tell when we have done so by the absence of the needed healing. By their fruits we shall know them.

Here is the clearest picture of the absolute relationship between authority and expectancy:

> When Jesus had entered Capernaum, a centurion came to him, asking for help. "Lord," he said, "my servant lies at home paralysed and in terrible suffering."
>
> Jesus said to him, "I will go and heal him."
>
> The centurion replied, "Lord, I do not deserve to have you come under my roof. But just say the word,

and my servant will be healed. For I myself am a man under authority, with soldiers under me. I tell this one, 'Go,' and he goes; and that one, 'Come,' and he comes. I say to my servant, 'Do this,' and he does it."

When Jesus heard this, he was astonished and said to those following him, "I tell you the truth, I have not found anyone in Israel with such great faith."

Matthew 8:5–10

A quick reading of this extract leads us to see that, yes, when a centurion gives orders, things happen! When Jesus gave orders, bondages were broken; demons were cast out; the dead were raised and the sick were healed! But let us also discover two interesting points here. Firstly, and this is of the utmost importance to a would-be healing minister, the centurion is suggesting that his own commands are carried out only because he himself is under authority. In the spiritual realm, as it is in any other walk of life, being positively and actively under someone else's authority is the only basis for exercising one's own; throwing one's not inconsiderable spiritual weight around without a deep sense of responsibility to God for one's actions can easily be quite abusive, if not heretical! Secondly, as the same story continues, in Matthew 8:13, Jesus says to the centurion, "'Go! It will be done just as you believed it would." And his servant was healed at that very hour.' Notice that Jesus was willing to go to the centurion's home; but the centurion's faith expectancy was rewarded as he saw heaven's grace fall much sooner. The servant was healed from that moment.

So what is the key to this spiritual authority? What is it that will make this expectant confidence work to the absolute glory of God, rather than serving only to make us look foolish, and disappoint the supplicant when things do not work out for them? If exercising our God-given authority to heal the sick in this most fruitful way is to work properly for the kingdom, then what will feed it? What will sustain it? What will give it holy substance? What will ensure that the power will follow?

There is an answer: ongoing devotion, and attendance to our sonship. We only have Christ's authority because we are, and want to continue to be, in a father/child relationship with God. This relationship is not only legal in nature, though it carries the very important aspect of inheritance, but it is, vitally, a relationship of love, which requires continuing attention. It needs to be growing ever closer. In terms of our relationship with God, though sonship, adoption by grace, is a given fact for the believer, there is an important sense in which we can never say to ourselves 'I have arrived!' We need to be moving ever more deeply into the amazing riches of our inheritance, growing more deeply in love with the Lord, more and more confident and aware of the reality and depth of his love for us personally. That is central to the great revelation of the New Testament. The love relationship made possible by the incarnation, God becoming man in Jesus, is the greatest gift of all:

> Everyone who believes that Jesus is the Christ is born of God, and everyone who loves the father loves his child as well.
>
> *1 John 5:1*

We learn from the story of the prodigal son that, through our adoption into his family, our Father has granted us the legal rights of sonship, calling for a robe, shoes and a ring before we have even re-entered the house. This reveals great truths. Shoes carry our bare feet, and barren hearts, from slavery into sonship. They are the sign that we are sons and agents of the estate owner, not like the barefoot slaves. In the gift of a robe is a mark of great honour. The ring is a sign of father-given authority. With the signet ring, estate policies may be signed, sealed and delivered, and orders given for the estate to be maintained.

As he sends us out into the harvest, the Father is reminding us that Jesus has been given authority over all things, and has shared that with us. We are sons with authority. There is a signet ring on every seat in every church; an offer, and an opportunity that needs to be taken.

In the putting into practice of this authority, the Christian may encounter some suspicion. The exercise of authority by the individual appears to the inexperienced eye to be on the wrong side of that fine dividing line between heresy and truth. To usurp Christ's authority without attending diligently to one's own sonship would indeed be heretical, but to move in authority, under his authority, remains a largely unexplored and forgotten truth, and most likely registers us in reactionary minds as being foolish; but we are 'fools for Christ's sake'. Fear not, for we are in good company! 'Fools' for Christ have always held a prophetic role in Christianity, from the early church until modern times. Such 'fools' in Christ sow the inevitable seeds of amazement, consternation and righteous anger that seem to follow out of necessity when Christ's work begins to be done among the worldly wise. Remember that the greatest measure of a minister is not his achievements but his willingness to step obediently out of the boat in response to the summons of Jesus, regardless of adversity and circumstances.

There have been many 'fools for Christ' down the centuries, and we all have our particular favourites, but often, in their time, they were considered to be verging on the insane —not, perhaps, in the psychiatric sense of the term, but in the 'nonsense' of what is holy; an 'insanity' to which any ordinary worldly sense of balance usually refuses to give any credit.

Do not be discouraged as you begin to move into the exercise of the appropriate delegated authority of a disciple of Jesus Christ. Holy perseverance in the use of authority is required of us. It has been said that truth usually passes through three phases. First, it is ridiculed. Secondly it is strongly opposed, and then, in the end, it is accepted as being self-evident. The truth in which we minister is founded on the clear mandate of the word of God, and there can be no stronger foundation.

We understand that everything has been put under the feet of Christ, and though we cannot yet see all the results of that, we can see dramatically more if we take hold of our authority and use it exactly as he taught disciples to do! As we go into the world with this *commanding* role, we must constantly remember that the son with the signet ring loses all credence with the estate workers and their problems if he does not attend to the maintenance of his sonship, his intimate knowledge of the estate owner's thoughts and will for the future. Taking care of sonship takes care of authority, and the power follows. The measure of it all will be the effectiveness of the ministry and all the glory going to God.

Setting out on such a freshly laid out ministry path with the Lord, we should become aware that, on either side of the track ahead, are two mighty, perilous ditches awaiting the unwary traveller. On the one hand is the pit of self pity and on the other is the ditch of self presumption. Both are easy to fall into. There will be disappointments on the way, expressed lack of belief, antipathy of leaders and still seemingly unanswered prayer which easily form a slip road down into the trough of self pity. There will be high excitements on the road as well; amazing miracles and great speaking invitations, which may trap us into believing, if only for a moment, that we are always right! This is the trap of the ditch of self presumption. We are the disciples; we are not the Master himself. We certainly do not keep moving along the way while we sit in either ditch, up to our waists in cold and filthy water!

6

A Fiercely Burning Flame

For myself, I can do nothing, in response to God's wonderful invitations to divine intimacy and provision, but pitch my life headlong into this healing ministry of the high King of heaven, so that others may have life and have it abundantly. The work of the kingdom of God is one of restoration, and his works are miraculous indeed.

In the background, behind the public face of the hospital and the local health clinic, there are scientists continuously pressing against the frontiers of knowledge. They need to fight disease with every new discovery that comes to them. There are new illnesses to battle against and old techniques and medicines that need to be enhanced.

I, on my parallel railway line of set-apart living devoted to Christ the healer, must push constantly against the boundaries of what is known in the church about the divine dispensation of healing gifts. Every new revelation might lead to another person being healed of their sickness. That is my ministry, to explore and then to advocate the thing I believe in, both in terms of the life I live and what I do.

As a minister of Christ's healing grace, there is only one place I can go to discover my role in helping others to benefit from the ever-open floodgates of the gushing river of heaven: the foot of his cross. Bible study, meditation and educational courses are all God-sent provisions, all building blocks of ministry, but the foundation of the building is always Jesus himself. There is no other place to begin, and no other person to return to.

Despite this certain knowledge of where to go, it feels, daily, that I am in no way properly and fully prepared for this work of grace, and therefore I have a tendency to assume that God's will in these matters could never be really brought to any fulfillment through me, although I am aware of the great error in this thought pattern, as it assumes that I actually do the healing and not Christ at work within me. Such hesitations are very common, but that does not excuse them!

Such lines of thought, however, may only serve to present most of us with an excuse, so that we are never prepared to start with the sick, or even to get ready to begin to minister. Our spirituality should tell us that there is more hidden in Christ than we shall ever learn. As long as we are prepared to study, we might as well begin the work. Happily, those of us who make an early start and begin to search the spiritual realms about this ministry are soon lifted up along the path ahead by fresh revelation.

I wonder if, then, the Lord is pleased with our enquiring efforts as we advance into unknown territory with him, troubled as he once was with the slowness of understanding in some of his original disciples. To suggest that we must wait for full divine impartation from heaven, or that we ought to know all the answers to all the questions that will be thrown at us, to wait to be invited to speak at a grand occasion, or to make sure that we will know all the thoughts and the directing of the Holy Spirit, seems to me to be, possibly, the shrivelled fruit of a lazy and worldly spirit. There is also another side to the same foolish coin: the minister who feels no need to search any deeper. He simply relies on the fact that the Son of God himself is our teacher about all these things as we go about through our life with him, giving to us of his own Spirit who reveals to mankind the deep things of God, imparting to us what we may call the mind of Christ. Wonderfully true though this undoubtedly is, a disciple must also be a student, and a student must always be searching for deeper things.

We Christians can fall into the trap of thinking that prayer (vital as it is) is a *substitute* for doing the work of the kingdom. Prayer is essential, of course, but when it is sometimes, mistakenly, spoken of as though it were an alternative to obedient action, then the nature of sonship, discipleship and delegated authority has been radically misunderstood. Claims to be praying about something when we know perfectly well we should be acting in obedience are nothing short of pharisaical. We are here *both* to pray *and* to do. We must either begin to do the work of the kingdom or share responsibility for the ineffectiveness of much of the church's ministry.

If we strive after full holiness, get ourselves properly prepared in every aspect of being a minister of Christ's healing, industriously giving our attention to going deeper in prayer and intercession, and get well grounded in his word, God helps us. Fear not, he will soon pour in his Spirit when we eventually reach the point of being prepared to let him minister his grace through us. There can be no doubt that what God gives us is to be given away to others, so his will is served by our freely giving what is given as soon as we receive it.

Who among God's caring people, deep down in their spirit, would not aspire to be a more prolific vehicle of this grace? Which one of us does not wish to live a life more devoted to, and guided by, the values that characterise the life and personality of Jesus? We really can live from day to day in such a brilliant and shining way that other people can find Christ through us. This, after all, is the role of the star that hung over Bethlehem, the travellers' guide to Christ.

To give light in the lives of others we must first have wisdom like that of the magi. We must start our journey by being drawn by the light of Jesus before we can ever reflect it. It was three wise men who went searching for Jesus at his nativity, and wise people are still seeking him today, looking to God's word for their direction. Although Bethlehem was a small town in those days, the Scriptures had said that out of it would come a ruler who would be a shepherd for his people Israel, and that is what happened. Those wise men had listened and obeyed that word, and it changed their lives, in the same way that it alters ours. They did not simply sit and pray for the coming of the Messiah; the moment came for action, and they did the right thing. They watched, listened and followed, and God rewarded their tireless obedience with the simple and awesome sight of his baby son, whom they could worship. What fantastic discoveries were made by those wise men because they acted in faithful obedience to God's word!

So much awaits us, such amazing joy, fruitfulness and blessing in serving, if we would only seek, then do, what the Lord has told us to do! Martin Luther once famously exclaimed, "The Bible is a great and powerful tree. Each word is a mighty branch. Each of these branches I have shaken well. And the shaking of them has never disappointed me."

As Christians learn to consider themselves potential ministers of healing grace, we should also learn to shake the branches of the Bible and allow God's revelation and blessings to shower down upon those we pray for, and us, as they did on the wise men of old in that first Epiphany story.

The would-be minister of healing grace will find layer upon layer of questionable philosophy along his way, built up and embraced by Christians over the centuries to excuse the supposed 'failures' of God in healing, and to avoid their having to stare at the frightening possibility that they may themselves be salt without savour.

The Bible has peace to soften perilous times, words of comfort to ease calamity, a word of light for the hour of darkness, and the assurance of healing in our pain. To the wounded soul and to the penitent heart it has a mother's reassuring voice and the pain relief that comes from her surrounding arms. While alive on this earth, none of us who knows this treasure to be their own remains barren and ravaged by life for long.

In approaching ministry for the first time, perhaps with some trepidation, especially when our trust weakens and it feels as though we trembling travellers are coming towards a grey valley of crushing scepticism, we take in both hands the rod and staff of Scripture and venture in, moving towards the lonely mountain pass of religious rejection and through darkness into the light of Jesus Christ. Today, wise men and women still rejoice in the message of God's word, and the earthward projected love of his Spirit, and worship him. On their eventual and first arrival at the house, the original magi saw the child with his mother Mary, and they bowed down and worshipped him. Then they opened their treasures and presented him with gifts of gold, frankincense and of myrrh. As, every day, we visit Jesus in the privacy of solitude and worship him, we demonstrate to our Heavenly Father, and to the world around us, that he is all our hope for this life and for eternity. As wise men we do well to proclaim: "Jesus loved me and gave himself for me. I dedicate my life to loving and serving him and to being a channel for his peace." But this is not still the first Christmas. The acclamation of the heavenly host is not heard, the star in the sky has retreated into the heavens, and the magi have gone home. The shepherds have long ago gone back to tending their sheep in the nearby fields. Now that the manger is empty and quiet, the work begins. Now wise men, too, must allow their Spirit-fired inspiration to carry them into mission.

Of course, we have to search out what we can with enquiring minds, but somehow we have to look for opportunities to find the lost, heal the broken ones, clothe the naked and feed the hungry. We have to rebuild the nations and bring peace among people. We have to befriend the lonely, set free the prisoner and, while we are about it, make music in all their hearts with the good news. This is the way of the healing gospel.

Stepping out with boldness onto the ministry road, there can be a temptation to fear, but only those who dare to risk can ever achieve great things. Anyway, none of us has anything more serious to do in this life than to reflect the light that will save souls. We can all therefore afford to spend our energies with enthusiasm, and be spent, in getting on with kingdom work.

The mountains that may appear to be set against us will move —if we do. When we have God-given passion and enthusiasm, we have the power to motivate and inspire. We can, with his help, succeed at anything for which God has given us unlimited passion.

Jesus of Nazareth is our witness to the meaning of enthusiasm: to be 'in God', to be full of his Spirit, to be in tune with the music of God's symphony of life, and to know his heart.

The Christ within us is passionately enthusiastic about the mission of establishing God's kingdom on earth (i.e. God's radical new order of things, in which he rules).

Faced with the breaking up all around us of nation societies with godly values, it becomes easy to be delighted about this kingdom way of being human in the world. To this in-God-ness, this kingdom enthusiasm, we should be prepared to subordinate everything else, to lead a life like a fiercely burning flame, totally consumed with this eagerness for the on-going establishment of the kingdom. We need to catch enthusiastic dis/ease in this broken and sinful world, and be centred on justice, compassion and salvation, especially for those most disadvantaged through poverty and ill health.

Any rightly motivated enthusiasm for ministry, and therefore any success at it, arises only out of a passionate commitment to God. So we must be inspired —no other motive will do. This deep, Jesus centred commitment of the soul will nourish our enthusiasm for people, and it will underline the redefinition of the nature of 'religious' faith.

A FIERCELY BURNING FLAME

Since the coming of Jesus Christ, the test or measure of religious commitment is not principally pious practice any longer. Its measure now is the practice of service with, and for, others.

The radical call of God on all Christians to follow this less travelled road of kingdom power, compassion and healing mercy is certainly something to be thrilled about! Through such divinely inspired exuberance, God promises that we will find and share life with others, now and for eternity! This passage reflects Jesus' own passion about this:

> Whoever finds his life will lose it, and whoever loses his life for my sake will find it.
>
> *Matthew 10:39*

First and foremost, the minister of God's healing grace must be completely assured of his calling. Ministry, in its simplest definition, is a matter of following what Christ is already doing, and, as he is doing countless kingdom works in the world, only prayer for revelation will discover the road ahead, the one on which he walks for us. The sharper the vision, the deeper the enthusiasm for it will be.

So pray we must. It would indeed be a sad day for each of us if we were to become absolutely contented with the religious life we lead, with the thoughts we think and with the deeds we do.

The finest days for any minister are those when there is, beating at the doors of his soul because he is still, in spite of everything else that ties him down, a child of God, a great longing to do something larger, something which he knows that he was made and meant to do. Could this

THE PASSION TO HEAL

be healing? Might it not be thrilling to carry a picture in one's mind of the cross of Christ being held against a gaping wound, and it being made whole again? That may be too fanciful for some, but compassion felt for others in their pain and suffering, when mixed with thoughts of the blessings of Calvary, will surely set the heart on fire!

Then, having felt, and grasped, the beginnings of our calling, we must accept that there is some danger in the storm ahead. Clasping what may still be only a watery vision, we set off in search of Christ among its waves.

Having stepped out in faith, Christ visits us with this strong assurance: "It is I, do not be afraid!"

The coming sense of his presence in our vision changes everything. It puts us into that place of spiritual confidence and courage where we can reply, "Lord, if it's you, tell me to come to you on the water."

Here, in our caution, we have a real desire to be with Christ in his mission but are still holding back. Without commandment we should rightly keep ourselves back from any unnecessary danger. Enthusiasm that is born of the spirit of the moment is often short-lived. Taking each step one at a time as Christ bids, we step out onto the water of our own vision for our ministry. The distance we will have to travel will turn out to be nothing; it is the first step that is a difficult one to take.

Although Jesus will remain in our line of sight, we will soon see a gust or two, then perhaps a storm will begin to blow up. We may become afraid, but then Christ will let us get on with our fearing, letting us sink, letting us cry, but then directing all our fears and cries to the right purpose. This fear of being swamped does not occur on dry land and serves wonderfully to shorten us to our knees in front of him. "Lord, save me!" we cry, and immediately, miraculously and unexpectedly, Jesus reaches out his hand and catches us. This is how God puts his searching children into his anointed ways, directing and protecting them. The love of Jesus Christ is constantly inclined towards us. Then we must follow him, stumbling through the potholes on the pilgrimage road behind the Lord, who strides out ahead saying, 'Everything is possible for him who believes,' and crying out to him, "I do believe; help me overcome my unbelief!"

Although this expectant belief is the base for effective ministry, there has to be more, much more. We cannot drive forwards against sickness and disease, with our child-like faith and delegated authority, if we ignorantly ignore our failures and things we do not yet understand. Triumphalists cannot expect to grow in ministry! Speaking out scriptural truths is often essential, but it is equally vital that, as we live and speak God's words, we are humble, compassionate, and full of the love of Jesus. Only then can we truly be 'water carriers for heaven'. We need to have drunk deeply of the love and grace that is to be found within the folds of the veil before we will know how to dispense it to others. Only so can the Christian use his authority and strength fruitfully.

Moreover, this enfolding cannot be a single occasion or some annual benefit. It must become a way of life. We must live our lives on the pilgrim road, within the veil. And we should concern ourselves less with what we tried and failed in, and far more with what it is still possible for us to do with God's help.

7

Into the Veil

Constantly seeking the presence of God is not a sort of technique for increasing his power or his willingness to heal the sick —Jesus healed all who came to him and it is in the nature of God to heal all those who come. Moses would leave the Lord's tabernacle, his face alight with God's presence in it, proving that presence to the people, who then came following God along their journey as a result. We who would minister today have to know the presence of God, so that those in need will come to Jesus for their healing. Even knowing his presence is not in itself enough. It is knowing, somewhere very deep inside, that his presence is a healing presence —not 'knowing' in any triumphalist sense, but in the deep humility and awe that come from living, day by day, in the certain presence of such power and love.

To increase our effectiveness in this way, to watch in awe with Peter as the sick are healed in our shadows, we must fall into being more Christ-like, more embedded in the veil's folds so that the permeating light affects us more and more. If our heavenly Father is the hand and Jesus is the touch, then the Holy Spirit within the veil is the 'burn'. In some mystical way, the healing pilgrim minister aches for this burn, not only because it is good to burn in the light of Jesus, but because it signifies that the journey must be getting ever closer to its source.

The healing minister must always be on the lookout for opportunities to lose his rough edges, and life on the pilgrimage road—the journey into the folds of the veil—can be a most abrasive grindstone. It can grind down, or polish up, the would-be pilgrim's reflective surfaces, depending, to a large extent, on what we are made of. Certainly, this 'life grindstone' of mine appears to have, from time to time, a most grating surface to it!

I seem to meander, day by day, in what frequently feels like an unguided fashion, across the vast and rolling landscape of the human terrain, together, I am sure, with other pilgrims on the discipleship road. We cross the high mountain ranges of God's 'love in action' with excitement, awe, revelation and mystery. We adventure on, with warming hearts, through the delicately swelling and gently breathing expanses of God's living presence in the ordinary and the everyday matters of our daily business. Somewhere out there on the road, however, as if to catch us when we are not looking, are the desert experiences of God, in which he deals with our human foibles. Out there are the deep and frightening chasms filled with that feeling of God's absence, resulting so easily and swiftly in patches of despair and loneliness.

It is in these times of despondency and hollowness, and especially in those seasons of creeping despair, that the pilgrim may experience an ever more powerful and swirling vortex, drowning out much of faith and far too much of hope. I suppose that this is the human equivalent of the collapsing star, the black hole whose mass increases to an incredible weight beyond anything previously dreamed of. In the long-term life of the true pilgrimage-making disciple, these are quite common experiences. They seem to be fired off inside us through a whole range of different human responses, particularly grief, over-tiredness, tragedy, hurt, disillusionment and burnout.

We should not be surprised by these sheets of black ice under our feet. To study the lives of great men and women is invariably to find that their greatness was developed, tested and then revealed in them through these emptier periods of their lives.

When I look back at my own journey as a Christian, it is easy to recognise that it was always in the days that followed contrary circumstances that my poor wisdom and understanding grew to new levels. It was in those times that I approached becoming the person I long to be.

One of the largest tributaries of the river of effective ministry is always the stream of adversity, full of the rocks of attendant pain. Happily, the grace of God is such that, in the confrontation between the stream and the rock, the stream always wins; not through strength but by perseverance. However, the assurance that there are always further depressions in the road ahead, as yet unseen, witnesses to the knowledge of God; the brook would lose its song if the rocks were all removed. The joyous flow of the Holy Spirit passing through our lives is only displayed in our changing.

I would never undertake such a Christian journey into ministry without friends; wanting to travel alone could be the outworking of an independent nature that subconsciously dislikes the idea of being an intricate and essential part of the body of Christ. If only because of our need for a corporate expectancy of God, such emotions would serve only to apply the brakes to our growth in ministry. There are many things that any of us can do on our own, but being a minister of God's healing grace is not one of them.

As the Christian life is, more than anything else, a state of union with Christ, and a union of his followers with each other, it follows that love among the community of Christ is inseparable from the love of God.

The personal relationship with Christ expressed in the dispensing of healing gifts can only be realised when one has begun to see oneself as a member of his Body, the Christian fellowship. Not just that —the making of this sort of pilgrimage requires some friends along the way who will reach down to help us to climb back out of our pits and hollows, and who can inject into us a refreshed desire for the road ahead, and an open-ness to the unknown territory that lies along the route.

In some kind of peculiar drifting from the abundant valley to the sterile desert, the pilgrim moves almost imperceptibly across some sort of frontier —a fine, intangible dividing line between hope and hopelessness, between a life full to its brim with the light and love of God and with vision, and one that is disastrously empty of any direction.

It is said that St. John of the Cross, imprisoned for his beliefs in complete darkness for nine months, was forced by virtue of his terrible surroundings into experiencing such a profound winter of the soul. He wrote that he felt himself to be impure and miserable; that he knew with sudden and enormous clarity that he was unworthy of God, or anyone else, for that matter.

Living unhealed, and yet as a minister of healing, I have shared momentarily in his desert place, in his emotion though not in his circumstance. I have often felt the need to cry out with the prodigal son, "Father, I have sinned against heaven and against you. I am no longer worthy to be called your son." But here is the miracle of these things: when the night is at its darkest, the eye begins to see.

Meanwhile, Saul was still breathing out murderous threats against the Lord's disciples. He went to the high priest and asked him for letters to the synagogues in Damascus, so that if he found any there who belonged to the Way, whether men or women, he might take them as prisoners to Jerusalem. As he neared Damascus on his journey, suddenly a light from heaven flashed around him. He fell to the ground and heard a voice say to him, "Saul, Saul, why do you persecute me?"

"Who are you, Lord?" Saul asked.

"I am Jesus, whom you are persecuting," he replied. "Now get up and go into the city, and you will be told what you must do."

The men traveling with Saul stood there speechless; they heard the sound but did not see anyone. Saul got up from the ground, but when he opened his eyes he could see nothing. So they led him by the hand into Damascus. For three days he was blind, and did not eat or drink anything.

In Damascus there was a disciple named Ananias. The Lord called to him in a vision, "Ananias!"

"Yes, Lord," he answered.

The Lord told him, "Go to the house of Judas on Straight Street and ask for a man from Tarsus named Saul, for he is praying. In a vision he has seen a man named Ananias come and place his hands on him to restore his sight."

"Lord," Ananias answered, "I have heard many reports about this man and all the harm he has done to your saints in Jerusalem. And he has come here with authority from the chief priests to arrest all who call on your name."

But the Lord said to Ananias, "Go! This man is my chosen instrument to carry my name before the Gentiles and their kings and before the people of Israel. I will show him how much he must suffer for my name."

Then Ananias went to the house and entered it. Placing his hands on Saul, he said, "Brother Saul, the Lord—Jesus, who appeared to you on the road as you were coming here—has sent me so that you may see again and be filled with the Holy Spirit." Immediately, something like scales fell from Saul's eyes, and he could see again. He got up and was baptised, and after taking some food, he regained his strength.

Acts 9:1–19a

The Apostle Paul—blinded for three days on the Damascus road—was given that time to travel across what must have been, and I can describe it from my own experience of losing my sight, one of the deep valleys that humans encounter. Surprisingly enough, it would have contained for him, as it did for me, the essential seeds of healing, deliverance and enlargement of belief for the new stages of his growth and discipleship that were to be called for in the unfolding days ahead of him. Those who wait for their healing (as I still do) would do well to ponder the lesson here: God was never the cause of affliction, but is wonderfully creative within it.

If we do not learn his lessons during our times of adversity, we have wasted the opportunity. Such hollows in the ground of our journey are part of the surface of the grindstone of life. In them we can battle depression and despair with the certain knowledge of Calvary's victory, and find there the ingredients for spiritual experiences and insights for the life of grace and truth to which all we Christians are called.

Looking back over the so-far travelled distance on my own pilgrimage road, I can see that the high peaks of my life were Spirit-drenched, but what of the plains and the valleys? I do not remember that those apparently Godless and dark grey, cloud-covered plains were anything to be particularly thankful for. The imaginative memory traces the path back down from the peaks of life to the specific valleys that join them. Peering through the fog with the eye of faith, they seem now to be a unified whole of antitheses and contrariety, everything revealing the mighty touch of God to the faith-focused eye.

Was gratitude there — in the troughs along the way? Life may hold fulfilment for us, growth and joy as we recall the finer places we have been to, and our senses may tell us that we are very happy with it, in the main. Pilgrim beware! Gratitude to God for past journeying, even on the peaks, can become misplaced, deflected, related in some way to the satisfaction with self and self's life. These scriptures can help us as we deal with this:

INTO THE VEIL

But Hezekiah's heart was proud and he did not respond to the kindness shown him; therefore the Lord's wrath was on him and on Judah and Jerusalem.

> Enter his gates with thanksgiving
> and his courts with praise;
> give thanks to him and praise his name.
> For the LORD is good and his love endures forever;
> his faithfulness continues through all generations.

Let the word of Christ dwell in you richly as you teach and admonish one another with all wisdom, and as you sing psalms, hymns and spiritual songs with gratitude in your hearts to God. And whatever you do, whether in word or deed, do it all in the name of the Lord Jesus, giving thanks to God the Father through him.

Do not be anxious about anything, but in everything, by prayer and petition, with thanksgiving, present your requests to God.

Be joyful always; pray continually; give thanks in all circumstances, for this is God's will for you in Christ Jesus.

Peace I leave with you; my peace I give you. I do not give to you as the world gives. Do not let your hearts be troubled and do not be afraid.

Then they worshipped him and returned to Jerusalem with great joy. And they stayed continually at the temple, praising God.

About midnight Paul and Silas were praying and singing hymns to God, and the other prisoners were listening to them.

You sympathised with those in prison and joyfully accepted the confiscation of your property, because you knew that you yourselves had better and lasting possessions.
So do not throw away your confidence; it will be richly rewarded.

2 Chronicles 32:25; Psalm 100:4–5; Colossians 3:16–17; Philippians 4:6; 1 Thessalonians 5:16–17; John 14:27; Luke 24:52–53; Acts 16:25; Hebrews 10:34–35.

We may have been siphoning off, for ourselves, the gratitude that should have been given to God. Failing to acknowledge the source of those ministerial, or just life-supporting, strengths within —the abilities, the care, the thoughts that have come—would be foolishness indeed.
In failing to point out to others the source of this strength, inspiration and love, we can, perhaps inadvertently, encourage them to admire the flowerpot instead of the flower within. Their ministries might suffer unnecessarily because of this, if they are unable to see that the strength for ministry within the Christian is just as much available to them as it is to us. The fragrance of humble and unselfish trust must find its way to us, and then, through us, to those others who God longs to bless.

INTO THE VEIL

Praise, on the flat plains and the hollow valleys as much as on the peaks, is the outward expression of that inner trust which keeps our eyes on the Father. It is a witness. It can be seen.

To turn around and walk on in trust is to leave the pothole behind. Scrabbling out of such a depression in the ground is often made easier through discarding our load of unnecessary and weighty baggage; left in the bottom of the pit, it lightens the climber, and we need others in the body to loosen the shoulder straps for us. For me, this is the way in which the realisation is often reinforced: that moving on through our pilgrimage necessitates the unshackling from our own backs of ways of thinking, misunderstandings and assumptions about life around us, its people, and the God we love and serve.

This walk is, put another way, like an unskilful servant who goes out into the garden to gather produce for the kitchen. He may collect many herbs, flowers and seeds, but on his return the owner of the house will only take from him what he finds to be useful today and throw the rest away. Jesus deals with our performances on the pilgrimage road in just the same way. He sifts out all the ingredients of self that are in them, adding incense to what he keeps, and then presenting what is good to the Father. In this way, Christ makes our growth into something more, and others are healed around us as we go.

Experiencing that winter season of the soul in his dungeon, St. John of the Cross came to see it as a necessary part of the journey of finding himself in God. This depth of soul darkness is one of the most impelling powers and pressures that drive us forward into the veil between heaven and earth.

It would seem that, once we have experienced this sort of cold soul-winter, during which it feels as though God has utterly turned his back on us, we can then more deeply ponder and experience the greatness of his love. Through constant meditation on the goodness of God, and on our amazing deliverance on Calvary from the punishment that our sins deserved, we are brought to realise our filthiness and utter unworthiness; that we did not deserve what was done for us on the cross. We begin to see that what we thought was the good we had done amounted to no more than a pile of filthy rags. We thank him that through his blood he has washed us clean and put on us the white robe of righteousness; and that that happened as a free gift, received by faith in the finished work of the cross when we came to Jesus.

In the Christian pilgrimage of discipleship, we begin to take on, more and more, the proper characteristics of God's children. We begin to walk in daily amazement with him, marvelling at his nature and his works. We constantly long after him and on our lips is an open profession of our faith in him.

8

The Scribe Becomes a Prophet

We may ask why we have to make such journeys, endure such spiritual hardships, and contemplate the need for such changes to self that are being called for here.

The answer is: salt and light, God's light. There is nothing we ministers can do to enhance the power to heal, because the work of the cross is complete. We can help considerably by keeping a sharp, biblical theology of healing in our hearts, but our main role in healing is to encourage the people to come. This is a sceptical and doubting world, and we need to reflect the light of Christ which draws the wondering seeker into his presence. It is there that healing begins.

Unhappily, whilst the church is filled with much prayer and much ministry, all is to a small effect, which comes nowhere near the pictures we enjoy of the early church, its joy, its peace of heart, and its power to heal. We have lost too much along the centuries, though much can be recovered through diligent discipleship. We are to be faithful to our Lord Jesus in persevering. There is great (albeit often dormant) power available for those who believe, and the nearer we live to him the more transparent we become to the oh-so-needed power flow of that mercy from heaven.

> I keep asking that the God of our Lord Jesus Christ, the glorious Father, may give you the Spirit of wisdom and revelation, so that you may know him better. I pray also that the eyes of your heart may be enlightened in order that you may know the hope to which he has called you, the riches of his glorious inheritance in the saints, and his incomparably great power for us who believe. That power is like the working of his mighty strength, which he exerted in Christ when he raised him from the dead and seated him at his right hand in the heavenly realms, far above all rule and authority, power and dominion, and every title that can be given, not only in the present age but also in the one to come. And God placed all things under his feet and appointed him to be head over everything for the church, which is his body, the fullness of him who fills everything in every way.
>
> *Ephesians 1:17–23*

Along the pilgrim road into the veil that separates us from our Creator, we begin to learn more about his ways. Together with all God's true children on that road, I remain constantly aware of my unworthiness to be there, having immense thankfulness for his mercies while I wait for, and rest in, his answers.

I wait in there, patiently under his hand, in obedience to

him, with what I trust is a heart ready and prepared, being sorrowful when thinking about my sinful nature, and with a sometimes painful sense of my own inadequacy.

Many would cheerfully take the opposite stand, spending all their lives in joyful acceptance of themselves as an example of God's miraculous making, which indeed we are. Others again may study diligently in search of God. However, entering into deep and intellectual discussions about, for example, the nature of the Holy Trinity, cannot be of any possible benefit to us if we lack humility, and offend the Trinity as a result. It is not our deep and wise deliberations that will make us holy and upright!

I would rather feel contrition than be intellectually skilful in defining that term. If I learned the whole Bible off by heart, it would all be of little value to me without knowing the love and grace of God permeating through my very bones. Living in the kingdom of God is both for this earthly existence and everlasting life. The kingdom is a vibrant, active spiritual organism, throbbing with authority and power, love, light and healing for all those who dwell within it.

Living in the kingdom of God does indeed have its benefits. Along the Christian pilgrim highway, we must all be encouraged to develop a continuous, and increasingly joyful, appreciation that, although sin and sickness still remain in our lives, they do not have the mastery over us. There is a very great difference between surviving sin and reigning sin; the new creation person battling with sin, and the ungodly soul who is complacent about it all. It is one thing for sin to live in us; it is another matter altogether for us to live in sin. It is one thing for sickness to live in us; it is another matter altogether for our lives to be ruled by it. Moreover, no-one can claim to have successfully avoided the 'yoke' of the religious life and claim that he is the sole judge of his own behaviour. We are accountable, above all, to our holy God; and to others within the body of Christ. It is vital that those who turn to us for ministry can have complete confidence as they look for consolation, advice, counsel and healing.

We must never be deceived by vain words or hopes, or false ideas about cheap or off-hand repentance. Often, in all sincerity, we express in prayer some deep sorrow and remorse for our shortcomings, using the most sorrowful and self-accusing language. At other times, we can become complacent about the presence of these things, notwithstanding our important sounding language of repentance. We must constantly be attentive to the voice of the Holy Spirit, who gently draws us to a position of humility and a readiness to repent as often as necessary, and keep short accounts with God.

The nature of the salvation of Christ can be grievously misrepresented by many present–day evangelists. They often focus on the work of our Lord in saving us from hell; less often, it seems, do they show us how he saves us from sin. So, many are disastrously misled. Many might wish to escape the Lake of Fire, yet have little desire to turn around to God and be delivered from the lordship of their worldliness. We shall never see the kingdom of God if, instead of seeking it here while we have the opportunity, we think of it only as a last place of sweet refuge into which we automatically enter at the end of sinful, self-centred lives. We cannot just make a cold, formal application for admission to heaven at the moment of death! The time to come to the cross is the present.

> But seek first his kingdom and his righteousness, and all these things will be given to you as well.
>
> *Matthew 6:33*

Words like repentance and holy living can only remain a sort of polite party-talk in church until we catch sight of enough of the deformity of our inward nature to be at least a little frightened at the sight of its evil character, if not quite terrified by it!

We can, of course, lead that outwardly credible form of the Christian life that has learned its traditional rules and style of religion by the use and custom of the centuries alone. This version of a religious lifestyle may often give the secure feeling of bringing the soul and the conscience to a place of rest and comfort for some time, even though all its inner roots and underground rivers of sin have never been shaken, nor even a little disturbed, by the garden fork of the Holy Spirit.

It is of the utmost importance that Christians should know that sin does not have the controlling lordship over us. Understanding this is of great help to us in our pressing onwards into the depths of sanctification. The full force of redeeming, regenerating and sanctifying grace has been brought to bear on us, and, through the Spirit, the centre of our moral and spiritual being has become the habitation of God. Christ has been formed in us, the hope of glory!

A life which has never tasted the bitter waters of repentance, and has only realised the need of a Saviour by second-hand witness, is sadly lacking. We must, sooner or later, with a broken and contrite heart, go to the cross of Calvary. He said, there, "It is finished." What was finished was his painful work of paying for our sin. We receive the benefit of his suffering when we truly accept what he did was for us personally.

This is surely the God to wonder at: the all-knowing, all-powerful and ever-present God, who wants to see his work of regeneration in every human life, and whose will is to sanctify those he has saved from sin. We pursue, and are pursued by, the God of infinite patience and love.

Here is our invitation to this intimacy, as the Lord comes to dwell in us, to be near, to hear us breathing, close enough to feel our pulse from within our hearts and to stand alongside our loneliness:

> O LORD, you have searched me
> and you know me.
> You know when I sit and when I rise;
> you perceive my thoughts from afar.
> You discern my going out and my lying down;
> you are familiar with all my ways.
> Before a word is on my tongue
> you know it completely, O LORD.
> You hem me in—behind and before;
> you have laid your hand upon me.
>
> *Psalm 139:1–5*

Such an invitation is not one to some kind of spiritual bed of warm cotton wool, that shelters us from the harsh effects of reality, but a hint of the miraculous grace of God whose greatest desire is that he should dwell in us and we in him.

Jesus, who searches and 'hems in' his creatures, knows us intimately, for: 'He did not need man's testimony about man, for he knew what was in a man' (John 2:25). Realisation of that truth astonished the Samaritan woman, amazed the Emmaus-road disciples, and fills me with wonder, too.

We modern day disciples might attempt to live as if we could banish this 'Sunday' God from our weekday unworthy thoughts, our prized bank balances and our tangled relationships, but did Jesus not come into our world, into our dark places, into our human scene with its hypocrisies and false values, its dirt and confusion? Let us acknowledge his glory and let him extend his lordship and let his light shine even over all the dark corners of our lives as he draws us into his presence along the pilgrim road, to know as we are known and to love as we are loved. 'Seven whole days, not one in seven, I will praise thee', wrote George Herbert (1593–1632).

While we humbly continue this pilgrimage journey, so much else will carry on easily and without much effort because of it. We find ourselves advancing along our chosen direction, feeling the presence of God. We experience his love, living in the enjoyment of his favour and in the hope of his glory.

In my own roadside hollows and even, occasionally, on the flat and open road, I sometimes sense that my prayers barely 'reach the ceiling'. But when I fall into this humble spirit by considering how good is the Lord, and how evil we all are, then I find that prayer mounts on new wings of faith expectancy to heaven. My helpless sighing, the groan of a broken heart for another traveller on the way, these things will soon go through the ceiling up to heaven and into the very bosom of God.

We must press on down this humble road into the Father heart of God. We will soon find, to our growing wonder, that all those past and present pains, disappointments, frustrations and discouragements, however insignificant they may have seemed before, become transferred through our prayer to God. The farther we go the more obvious this becomes—our pains seem to fall into him. Once there, because of his self-emptying and enfolding love—we discover that they are infinitely more unpleasant to him than they ever were to us.

I can only suppose that God is prepared to carry all our discomfort like this for the sake of some goodness he foresees for us, and, above all, because he loves us. I am more than willing to take the view that, should I fall into such a roadside depression as we have been describing, it will be a place for me to learn more of what God suffers. If I can take what comes to me in that hollow place through him, then bitterness changes to sweetness and great darkness is transformed into clear light. It is almost as though everything begins to take its flavour from God.

When our thoughts can function in that mind-set, everything that happens to us in life reveals God a little more to us. All things drift into having this one taste: the presence of our Holy God.

It follows, quite naturally, that God becomes the same to us in life's sweetest pleasures and bitterest moments alike. His nature never changes. We begin to see that the ups and downs of our feelings, our faith, our journey, do not reflect any change in God, who is always the same, yesterday, today and forever; absolutely loving and dependable.

So what of this re-shaping and re-colouring of our individual book of life —is it of benefit to the church?

The modern church, whatever its branch and style of spirituality, is battered by the harsh voice of our scribes, while the people cry out for the tender tongues of the prophets, to teach them the realities of God. There is an essential difference between those tendencies that I characterise under the terms 'scribe' and 'prophet'. The scribe simply repeats to others what he has heard or read about. Such knowledge is good and often fruitful in itself, but does not enable any healing experience of the love of God to be ministered to another; that grace is granted only to those who have a burning and tender love for him, often forged in the potholes of life. Even the worldly, the unconverted, may possess the 'scribal' kind of knowledge, yet without knowing God and the reality of his love for themselves. There is power in the word of God, of course, but the scribe who has not learnt to minister the word in compassion, under the anointing of the Holy Spirit, will be an ineffective minister. Factual knowledge is too often administered like cold, tasteless water to God's children. But if those who find in themselves that 'scribal' tendency will humbly go to our Lord in repentance and ask for his forgiveness and for the Holy Spirit, he will turn their water into wine and empower them to become fruitful.

The prophet, unlike the scribe, has seen, felt and tasted the saving heart of God for his people, and comes warmly to us, to relate what he has understood from that experience. With outstretched hands, the prophet speaks of the depths of love that he has found, deep in the folds of the veil between heaven and earth. It is in the relating that follows that healing flows. This gushing fountain of divine love comes only from our Lord himself. No one who thinks of Jesus as a stranger can even begin to understand the immensity and attraction of that amazing love.

Effective authority in kingdom ministry does not flow from what we say, what prayers we use, or from how we dress and behave in church; it issues from what we are, and what we are is governed by our relationship with God himself. The scribe can only tell us stories *about* the kingdom. The prophet brings it with him, and invites us to go in.

> If I have the gift of prophecy and can fathom all mysteries and all knowledge, and if I have a faith that can move mountains, but have not love, I am nothing.
> *1 Corinthians 13:2*

9

His Approaching Footsteps

We should beware. It is so easy for a prophet, as we have described him, to fall back into the role of a scribe. A vision not upheld is an easy vision to lose.

One of the deepest pitfalls on the road that continually faces us—perhaps especially we Christian ministers—is that we can become so preoccupied with the doing of God's work that we can easily slip unnoticed up the side track of forgetting about him while we do it. It is then that we will only have the minutes with God to be scribes and never the hours with him out of which we might prophesy.

We may self-defensively argue, under our breath, that Jesus has left us a great deal of work to do. We do, after all, have a duty to him and to the church to preach his word and visit the needy. As if that is not enough, we must comfort those who are oppressed, fight injustice and tear down evil strongholds; whilst we carry out many other tasks, reflecting the range of gifts and anointings that are given for service in the kingdom. All the while that we are doing this, we must stress and demonstrate that evil need never be victorious and declare that Jesus is alive!

I find, for my own part, that ministry can readily turn into mere busyness, rather than Holy Spirit directed work. The sign I came to recognise that I had turned off the track was the temptation to force prayer into the back seat. "I can do nothing," I have been guilty of saying on a few past occasions, "I can only pray." Putting it like that tends to suggest that prayer is a rather insecure, probably unreliable, second-best option. Those to whom I ministered might well have concluded that I would only have some hope to offer if I could work and worry and rush back and forth. Practical help is fine, but we must beware of unintentionally suggesting that prayer is a desperate option that we fall back on only when we run out of practical measures and things are getting critical!

Over the years, I have discovered that I need to be robustly reminded, day by day, that the Christian healing ministry is his labour, not mine, and that he has asked me to be his partner in his ongoing work of redemption. But I cannot give what I do not have. What I am called to give—rather, *who* I am called to give—is what comes from God himself: his compassion, love, healing mercy, and his listening. If I do not know him, I cannot communicate and share any true knowledge of him.

I can, of course, grow to know him a little through his creation, through study, through reading Scripture and by interacting with others. I have found these to be useful helps in approaching God, but there is one way to know him better which is essential: prayer.

This in itself carries its own concerns. I am afraid that we might have too often taught our people to use ministry and prayer as a means of ease and consolation—hardly in the original and stalwart sense of restoration, inspiration and strengthening, but more in the shallower and baser sense of soothing sorrow, dulling pain and drying tears. This is the comfort of the cushion and not the comfort of the cross. No, we need the prayer that leads us to Calvary; to find a way to share, through his death the way to become more Christ-like, more filled with God, and more self emptying than ever before. This is how we truly and deeply give the things of God to others.

This may all appear at face value to be self-evident, but if I am critically honest with myself, I know that busyness can sometimes force prayer sideways out of my way and out of my day. The prayer with the congregation and the supplications of ministry may remain, but the prayer which is my Lord and I alone together can be forced further and further to the limits of my life, and, on one most regrettable, though thankfully rare, day or another, simply and quietly disappear. When it does, there is left in its place an aching sense that the whole religious life might just be empty and artificial.

For me, glorifying God has become the great work that I am more than ambitious of achieving, and increasing time spent with him in the most delightful privacy only serves to deepen my strong affection towards the Godhead, and so I find myself, more often than not, in private with him. I hunger for our time of meeting with each other, many times a day, to talk over my life with him, my desires and disappointments, my doubts and my strivings. Communion with God, it must be said, is the strongest need in my soul. I find, in these moments, the total reassurance that I am alive only for God. It is here that I recognise Christ to be nearer to me than mother or father, any close relation, or even the most affectionate of my friends. It is in this recognition that I rejoice to love him and to follow him. Communion with God is what I was created for. Prayer is the beginning of that communion, and any daily need may be the motive that creates the prayer. The sole design of prayer is that it should be a togetherness, a talking with God, a coming-to-one with him.

Of course, I must ask before I can receive what I want to give away —but receiving what I ask for in respect of my own smaller needs is not God's purpose in bringing me to his knee to pray; he could give me everything without my having to ask for it. God withholds that man may ask— prayer brings his child to his knee, not to whine or to coldly present a shopping list, but to stand in the warmth of his peace and to feel his presence. So I continue, in my silent prayers of private communion, not in order to try and possess his gifts, but just because he *is* true life. I need to be quiet; listening and waiting in my sinfulness and his forgiveness, and in this way I have learned that the silent company of God is most often more healing than a thousand words of human advice.

I need him to be my strength in my weakness. He longs to be present to me in the way that I need it, perhaps in a different way each day, and then I need to let him be the healing God in the way he wills, working through me.

I need no holy wings to fly to high mountains in search of him; I need only to find a place where we can be alone together, and I can look upon him, deep within me.

The crucial question for me has always been whether I should pray fairly continuously or at certain times of the day, and whether or not any particular type of prayer is necessary. In the end, so much time is spent drifting in and out of the veil—continuously flowing back and forth between the vagaries and the falsehoods of the world and the truth within the veil—that I almost cease to give prayer at all. I can safely say that my life itself is becoming a prayer. Even the act of intercession for some needy soul becomes the simple act of carrying that soul with me into the veil.

If I admit to myself that it is good to turn to God in prayer when and as I can spare the time, or advise someone with a problem to take their refuge in prayer, I am as good as confessing that praying is one of the activities on the margin of my life, and that therefore, by implication, it does not really matter. How could we ever suggest this?

Prayer, at its best, is nothing more than holding a quiet conversation with God who loves us. It should be the sum of our relationship with him.

We are what we pray. The extent of our faith is the extent of our prayer, and our ability to love other people is entirely governed by our ability to pray. Prayer does not need to be enthusiastic and ecstatic to place us deeply enough in his power, and at his disposal, that nothing is held back from us. Neither does it have to be filled with blissful jubilation, or that wonderful brilliance of carefree surrender. Indeed, my own prayers feel sometimes as though I have some kind of slow internal haemorrhage, where grief and sorrow for the afflicted ones that have come recently across my path seem to make my inner heart's-blood leak away silently into God's unfathomed depths. Prayer within the healing ministry is not often a bandage —it is most often the wounded Christ within, sharing the hurt, the human pain.

Surrounded as we are by the values of this modern

world, we might be tempted to believe that silence brings death to communication because it disrupts and denies social interchange. Social interchange, however, is not essential in this prayer life in the folds of the veil. Quietness between man and God means that there is nothing in the nature of babbling request. Silence in the company of other human beings is often difficult and sometimes well-nigh impossible!

But when Jesus Christ became man, he gave perennial value, and a new meaning, to solitude. His loneliness on the mountainside and, for different reasons, in Nazareth, gave us a meaningful insight into his closeness to his Father. In those quiet places, Jesus found the courage to follow Father God's will, to speak the Father's words and do his works.

> By myself I can do nothing; I judge only as I hear, and my judgment is just, for I seek not to please myself but him who sent me.
>
> *John 5:30*

> Don't you believe that I am in the Father, and that the Father is in me? The words I say to you are not just my own. Rather, it is the Father, living in me, who is doing his work.
>
> *John 14:10*

> Going a little farther, he fell to the ground and prayed that if possible the hour might pass from him. "*Abba*, Father," he said, "everything is possible for you. Take this cup from me. Yet not what I will, but what you will."
>
> *Mark 14:35–36*

HIS APPROACHING FOOTSTEPS

It was in the lonely, silent and shimmering heat of the wilderness, too, where Jesus' earthly ministry grew out of the inner communion between the Father and himself, the Son. It is there for us, too, all alone and waiting with him in the silent places, that all is made ready; and then his will to heal becomes more evident through our ministry.

It is now in this private place that I can do nothing but beseech him to ride on triumphantly as I lay my proud thoughts and desires across his path, quietly shouting, "Hosanna! Welcome to my heart!"

In there he has another temple waiting for him, quite as precious to him as the original. Like that other holy place in Jerusalem, my heart is full of sin, as thieves and robbers make their home there. In hesitant and humble prayer, I urge him to enter my heart's doors and crucify the evil to be found within, so that the floor of the temple may be cleansed for the passing of his feet.

If, then, for some unknown reason, I still cannot find the words to live another day of praise, then I still have his reassurance that the very stones that make the walls of my heart's temple will cry out, "Hosanna!", as the trembling heart lives in the expectancy of hearing the sound of his approaching footsteps. And when he comes, what then?

> Not until halfway through the Feast did Jesus go up to the temple courts and begin to teach. The Jews were amazed and asked, "How did this man get such learning without having studied?"
> Jesus answered, "My teaching is not my own. It comes from him who sent me."
> *John 7:14–16*

In some mysterious and God-fired way, as Christ in his Spirit impresses his love and compassion over and over again into our hearts, our teaching ceases to be our own. It comes from him who is sending us. That compassion of his crosses the distance between the captive heart and the hurting soul that God brings to be alongside it.

> A man with leprosy came to him and begged him on his knees, "If you are willing, you can make me clean."
> Filled with compassion, Jesus reached out his hand and touched the man. "I am willing," he said. "Be clean!"
> Immediately the leprosy left him and he was cured.
> *Mark 1:40*

In his compassion, he heals the sick. If we truly want others to be physically and emotionally at peace in Christ, we must practise compassion. If we want to be ourselves in that very same state, then we must practise compassion.

10

The Kiss of Tender Healing

The ministry of divine healing remains today in a quandary. In the early days of Christianity it was a real force for healing in the world. Nowadays, those who support and practise it are often seen only as the purveyors of some strange jiggery-pokery.

Thankfully, much vital work continues today in other fields of wholeness: counselling, listening, the provision of retreat houses, and many more aspects of the ministry. The actual healing of sickness itself has, with the exception of a few valiant preachers in spiritual 'hot spots', fallen largely into disarray.

Well, we say, we have our medical profession these days, and some alternative treatments may be useful. Christian healing sometimes seems to be clinging on to the edge, with ever decreasing strength in its fingernails.

In so many New Testament passages it is attested over and over again that the healing of the sick through the laying on of hands was understood as normative, and common practice, in the first generation of Christians. How my heart so longs to go back to those days! How much I yearn for the reality of God's love to freely manifest itself among the body of Christ in grace! God has not changed. Sickness is as loose in the world as it always was. What has changed is our attitude towards it all.

But it is a long way back to that era. Centuries have gone by. Much of what was spiritual has become thought of as superstitious; what was a Spirit-led lifestyle has, to a large extent, been replaced by legalism, ritualism and formalism, without the softening and love-comprehension of the Holy Spirit, who inspired the word. What was the expectancy of divine intervention has been supplanted by considerable scepticism, and what had a corporate nature has become a gathered group of individuals. Harsh though this observation might seem, the recognition of truth is a fine foundation for forward movement. The truths of the Bible will help us to find the way. Vast numbers of people throughout the world, whatever their spiritual, emotional, mental or physical condition, have found blessed relief and cure because of them.

However, as ministers of his grace, we must be always dissatisfied with our effectiveness. Of course, there is in the end the mystery of Almighty God, but let us push the evil of sickness under the feet of Christ's authority as much as we may, before allowing our responsibility as authorised disciples to die away from lack of understanding, labelling problems—that often stem from our own ignorance and unwillingness to act—to be ascribed to his mystery.

If the whole church were involved with the sick to the same degree and magnitude as our medical services, it would still not be enough. It is not adequate only to

THE KISS OF TENDER HEALING

intercede for people, valuable as that is; it is much better to go further and exercise our God-given authority and sonship on their behalf. How far can we go? How long must we press on into this ministry? Have we any human role model for our ministry growth? How far into the things of God do we need to advance?

> As a result, people brought the sick into the streets and laid them on beds and mats so that at least Peter's shadow might fall on some of them as he passed by. Crowds gathered also from the towns around Jerusalem, bringing their sick and those tormented by evil spirits, and all of them were healed.
>
> *Acts 5:15–16*

When the sick that lie in our shadows—all of them—are healed, then perhaps we will begin to honour our inheritance, and the Lord who included us in his living and working body.

Wherever our individual ministries are today, whether just starting out or highly experienced, the way onwards is into a life of prayer. It is through prayer that we can approach hitherto untapped resources of power, not through intercession *per se*, but through leading the life of prayer. It is the desire for such a life that empowers the body afresh for 'greater things than these'. When Jesus' disciples failed to heal the demonised boy, he addressed this very concern,

> But Jesus took him by the hand and lifted him to his feet, and he stood up.
> After Jesus had gone indoors, his disciples asked

him privately, "Why couldn't we drive it out?"

He replied, "This kind can come out only by prayer."

Mark 9:27–29

Somewhere deep down inside, I know that, without a lonely place, my life as a minister is in danger of being lost altogether. Most of us in the church's healing ministry today would have much in common with those disciples who could not deliver the demonised boy —we have too many failures with no reasons why. Somewhere I know that, with all the authority in the world, but without listening silence, our actions quickly become empty gestures, words lose their meaning, and speaking in authority, as they discovered, no longer heals.

The careful balance between silence and words, withdrawal and involvement, solitude and community, is a twisted thread of gold entwined into the basis of the Christian life. Without it, we will know all the words, sing all the notes, and yet still not know the song. We may know something intellectually from our head down, and intuitively from the soles of our feet up, and yet not deep in our hearts. Since we should always take our instruction from the words and actions of Jesus, we must discover a space for silence if we are to follow him —no matter how much our neighbour's needs may draw on our time and drain away our energy. Psalm 139:1–5 is all our invitation to intimacy, as God comes to dwell in us, to be near, to hear us breathing, to feel our pulse and to stand alongside our loneliness.

There are many other and different ways in which Christ can express his love in and through me, but there has to be a listening to him if my life is to be Christ–like, and allow the lives of others to be affected by the power of his cross. Christian listening is not the titillation of curious ears, it is a fundamental lifestyle of waiting on the Lord and a laying open of the heart to his prompting and direction.

For some, there are times when prayer can seem irksome and any excuse to have to by-pass it welcome. Then, a feeling of relief falls over the rest of the day when it is over. Reluctant to begin, we may be delighted to finish. While at prayer, any trifling diversion can be enough to distract our attention. This not uncommon attitude should not be shocking —the fact that prayers were, in some traditions, set as penances tells its own story. Yesterday's prayers may well have been full of joy, thanksgiving and exaltation, and yet today's can, to some degree, seem like a burden.

It does not disquieten me so much that, under such circumstances, I have, at one level, a desire to cut short and begrudge the duty of prayer. The most troubling thing is that, in the past, I have even thought of prayer at all as being one of my duties, because I was created to glorify God and enjoy him forever. (See Romans 15:6,9.)

Still waters alone have the depth for God to fill with himself.

> He makes me lie down in green pastures,
> he leads me beside quiet waters.

> The purposes of a man's heart are deep waters,
> but a man of understanding draws them out.

> In your anger do not sin;
> when you are on your beds,
> search your hearts and be silent.
> Offer right sacrifices
> and trust in the LORD.

Very early in the morning, while it was still dark, Jesus got up, left the house and went off to a solitary place, where he prayed.

Then he returned to his disciples and found them sleeping. "Could you men not keep watch with me for one hour?" he asked Peter. "Watch and pray so that you will not fall into temptation. The spirit is willing, but the body is weak."

"But when you pray, go into your room, close the door and pray to your Father, who is unseen. Then your Father, who sees what is done in secret, will reward you."

"Come to me, all you who are weary and burdened, and I will give you rest."

Psalm 23:2; Proverbs 20:5; Psalm 4:4–5; Mark 1:35; Matthew 26:40–41; Matthew 6:6; Matthew 11:28.

Jesus calls us from loneliness to solitude. If loneliness may be described as being inner emptiness, then solitude is inner fulfilment. It is not primarily a place but a state of mind and heart. The purpose of being in silence and solitude is to be able to see, hear and soak into the things

THE KISS OF TENDER HEALING

of God. It is not easy for any human being to keep the eyes open while the mouth and ears are working!

Any actions of Jesus were preceded by prayer in solitude, and then those actions were most powerfully effective. Firstly, he had to be both rested and sure of the Father's will. Then he led us in the way that we are called to follow: teaching, healing and demonstrating, to those with eyes to see, the in-breaking of the kingdom of God.

> One of those days Jesus went out to a mountainside to pray, and spent the night praying to God. When morning came, he called his disciples to him and chose twelve of them, whom he also designated apostles: Simon (whom he named Peter), his brother Andrew, James, John, Philip, Bartholomew, Matthew, Thomas, James son of Alphaeus, Simon who was called the Zealot, Judas son of James, and Judas Iscariot, who became a traitor.
>
> He went down with them and stood on a level place. A large crowd of his disciples was there and a great number of people from all over Judea, from Jerusalem, and from the coast of Tyre and Sidon, who had come to hear him and to be healed of their diseases. Those troubled by evil spirits were cured, and the people all tried to touch him, because power was coming from him and healing them all.
>
> *Luke 6:12–19*

Jesus needed inner quiet and now he offers it, in his great grace, to us. When I think of this inner peace, there springs up in me the image of a deep rock pool, high in a distant mountain range, filled with the placid clarity of ice-cold fresh water, not the foul stagnation of an old roadside puddle, drying and cracking in the midday sun.

My times of inner quiet are far from being born out of a complacent acceptance of 'fate'; it is no resignation on my part in the face of hardship, no escape from the realities of life around me —it is simply a still point of the spinning world, a deeply creative and motivating time for reflection in a world full of action.

In whatever ways that any of us are called to the service of our Lord, such a release from outer stress and inner strife were surely never more needed than they are today. I have found for myself that locating and nurturing this inner resource of the Spirit is utterly essential for effective ministry, and for what I trust to be flourishing Christian discipleship.

This is kingdom living, and the kingdom of God is located within. It is in settling myself down in solitude that I come upon him in myself.

> Examine yourselves to see whether you are in the faith; test yourselves. Do you not realize that Christ Jesus is in you—unless, of course, you fail the test?
> *2 Corinthians 13:5*

Quietness before the Lord and in his kingdom becomes a tool for carving out a warm cave of inner stillness so that, while we sit peacefully inside it, the Holy Spirit can be heard, and the conscious and sub-conscious confines of the mind can be brought into harmony with each other. That certain deep stillness, in a place and time not cluttered by physical noise, cerebral musings and diversions or emotional stress, is where the Holy Spirit heals, creates, renews, refreshes and inspires. These are good times to be alone with him.

THE KISS OF TENDER HEALING

I stood alone like this in front of God when he first called me and I had to answer that call on my own. It is on my own that I have to struggle and pray through that calling, and it will be alone, in the end, that I will have to die and give an account of my life to him. If I try to live in the world as though only God and my soul were in it, and that is the effect of a life spent on the pilgrim road into the veil, all family, possessions and ministry become seen merely as gifts from him. These are wonderful gifts to be sure but, in the end, only gifts.

At least I have the assurance that my heart will never be enslaved by any earthly thing.

I cannot escape from myself because God has singled me out to minister to his people. When I refuse to be alone with him I am rejecting the call of Christ to me.

To be calm and quiet in this fashion, all by myself, is quite the opposite of sleeping. In fact, it involves being fully awake and following, with the closest attention, everything going on inside. Important here is an underlying wisdom and self-discipline which recognises the urge to move swiftly onto some other task as being a temptation to look elsewhere for what is really close at hand.

Silent prayer is the opening of the hands before God, slowly relaxing the tension of worldly living which tightly clasps them together, and accepting one's own existence with an increasing readiness, not as if it were some hilltop position to be defended, but as a gift to be continuously received.

Prayer, then, should be a way of life for the minister of healing, that allows us to find a stillness in the middle of the rushing world, where hands can be opened to God's promises, finding healing for oneself, one's fellows and the whole surrounding community.

It is only from being hidden away with him in the secrecy of the heart that we have the courage to go, and know that the Lord goes with us. He leads us each day, if we will allow it, into the quiet place of each heart, where he will always speak with us. For my part, I know that from there he blesses and watches over me —that he listens to me in his gentle understanding, and that he is with me always, wherever I am and however I may be feeling.

It must be emphasised here that stillness and quiet, space to have freedom from the demands of others, and becoming inwardly directed, are not goals in themselves. They are only stepping stones on the way across the river of human ignorance and ineffective ministry to the far bank of learning the meaning of God's love for us, learning to live in it, and learning to dispense it to those who need it. As one finds the reality of that love, it becomes possible to offer oneself to God in a mature way and to give some of the same love and understanding to others, that self-emptying love of Jesus with no strings attached.

Whatever else it might involve, I have found in this process of growing in peace and in solitude the meaning of my having been born again, of giving up an old life and being given a new one.

It is out of such quiet places that ministry becomes anointed with heaven's authority. All outward power that we can exercise in the situations around us is only a shadow when compared with that inner power from the Holy Spirit that dwells in, and fires up, our desire to bless others.

Prayer, when it is the prayer of expectancy, the prayer of the heart, opens us afresh to God's creating and recreating power, forming and healing the soul and the body into everything that the desire of our spirit reaches after.

Corporate prayer marked by expectant faith is graciously used by God: we see him open the kingdom of heaven and unlock the treasure chests of the riches of Christ, including healing of the sick. We are refreshed, and brought into a deeper experience of communion with the Lord. Then, when we heal the sick, we do it together —a joint ministry between heaven and earth that glorifies Jesus Christ and satisfies the needy. His will is done. His kiss of tender healing breaks through.

*More books by the same author,
published by Terra Nova Publications Ltd:*

HEALING AT THE WELL
ISBN 1901949079
£7.99   Canada $19.95   New Zealand $29.95

TRUST YATES!
Stories of a Guide Dog with a Dog Collar
ISBN 1901949087
£5.99   Canada $14.95   New Zealand $22.95

FIND THE WAY!
More Stories of a Guide Dog with a Dog Collar
ISBN 1901949168
£6.99   Canada $16.95   New Zealand $26.95

LET HEALING FLOW, LORD
ISBN 1901949141
£8.99   Canada $22.95   New Zealand $33.95

HEAVEN'S DYNAMITE
God's Amazing Power to Heal the Sick
ISBN 1901949214
£7.99   Canada $19.95   New Zealand $29.95

Available from Christian bookshops, and online from:

www.amazon.co.uk *and*
www.jacobswell.org.uk

Available in Canada from:
www.anglicanbookcentre.com

Available in New Zealand from:
CLC New Zealand, Feilding